PREFACE

An increasing amount of attention has been given in recent years to the civilization of the Byzantine Empire, which flourished in the Greek East from the early part of the third century A.D. to 1453. Although many learned works have been written about that great Christian civilization, still certain important aspects of it have been but little explored. This is especially true of its philosophy and theology, and the deeper essence and significance of its art.

Since 1949, I have done considerable research in the fields of Byzantine art, philosophy and theology, and from time to time have published the results of my research. In this volume I have gathered together some of my already published articles and have added three papers that have not appeared in print: "Philosophy," "The Way to Knowledge," and "Hymnody."

The first essay — "Philosophy" — is a lecture which I delivered before the philosophy students of Tufts University, Medford, Massachusetts, on April 5, 1965. The third essay — "Conscience" — is an article which appeared in St. Vladimir's Seminary Quarterly, June, 1965. Chapter Four — "The Philokalia" — is an article which appeared in Jubilee, October, 1961. Except for the long concluding paragraph, the fifth chapter — "Aesthetic Examination of Byzantine Art" — is a paper which I read at the meeting of the Southern Society for Philosophy and Psychology at Knoxville, Tennessee, on April 11, 1952, and which was published by Athene, in the summer, 1953 issue. The sixth chapter — "Iconography" — is a somewhat revised version of the Introduction of my book Byzantine Sacred Art: Selected writings of the contemporary Greek icon painter Fotis Kontoglous (New York, 1957). With the exception of the last paragraph, the seventh essay — "Manuel Panselinos" — has been taken from my book *Anchored in God: Life, art, and thought on the Holy Mountain of Athos* (Athens, 1959). Chapter Eight — "El Greco and Byzantine Painting" — is an article which appeared in *Ekklēsia* (Athens), August, 1964, while Chapter Nine is the chief part of my booklet *Byzantine Sacred Music,* which was published in 1956.

Inasmuch as I use over a hundred transliterated Byzantine terms and English translations of them, I have deemed it useful, for readers of the theological-academic world, to append a Greek-English and an English-Greek glossary.

In transliterating common nouns, adjectives and so on, I have followed the method used by English scholars. In translating proper names I have retained the *-os* ending, instead of using *-us,* which obliterates the distinction between Greeks and Latins. Thus, I have written Athanasios instead of Athanasius, Dionysios instead of Dionysius, and so on. Otherwise, I have, in general, followed the conventional modern English translations of proper names.

I am grateful to the editors of the above mentioned journals for permission to republish the respective articles that appeared in them; to Professor Pal Kelemen, for providing photographs of two illustrations contained in his book *El Greco Revisited* and giving me the permission to use them in the present volume (Figs. 14 and 18); and to Dr. John Johnstone, Jr., for reading the entire manuscript and suggesting many improvements in expression.

CONSTANTINE CAVARNOS

CLARK UNIVERSITY
WORCESTER, MASSACHUSETTS
January, 1968

BYZANTINE THOUGHT AND ART

Christ the Pantocrator. Detail. Early XIth century.
Mosaic in the Church of Hosios Lukas, Boeotia.

BYZANTINE
THOUGHT AND ART

A COLLECTION OF ESSAYS

BY

CONSTANTINE   CAVARNOS

INSTITUTE FOR BYZANTINE
AND MODERN GREEK STUDIES
115 Gilbert Road
Belmont, Massachusetts

CONTENTS

PREFACE   vii

I   PHILOSOPHY   13

II   THE WAY TO KNOWLEDGE   30

III   CONSCIENCE   40

IV   THE *PHILOKALIA*   48

V   AESTHETIC EXAMINATION OF BYZANTINE ART 59

VI   ICONOGRAPHY   73

VII   MANUEL PANSELINOS   79

VIII   EL GRECO AND BYZANTINE PAINTING   85

IX   SACRED MUSIC   97

X   HYMNODY   109

        NOTES   116

        GLOSSARY   127

        INDEX   135

ILLUSTRATIONS

Christ the Pantocrator, Church of Hosios Lukas, Boeotia. Mosaic. Frontispiece

1 Church of Hagia Sophia, Constantinople. Exterior. 62

2 Church of Saints Theodore, Athens. Exterior. 63

3 Capital, Church of Hagia Sophia, Constantinople. 65

4 Church of Saint Demetrios, Thessaloniki. Exterior. 66

5 Church of Saint Demetrios, Thessaloniki. Interior. 67

6 Church of Hagia Sophia, Constantinople. Interior. 68

7 Saints Basil and Gregory Nazianzen, Church of Kaisariani, near Athens. Fresco. 69

8 Saint Barlaam, Monastery of Barlaam, Meteora. Fresco. 71

9 The Holy Virgin Mary and the Child Christ. Panel icon by Kontoglou. 75

10 Saint Procopios, Church of the Protaton, Mount Athos. Fresco by Panselinos. 80

11 Saint Theodore Tyro, Church of the Protaton. Fresco by Panselinos. 81

12 Saint Theoktistos, Church of the Protaton. Fresco by Panselinos. 83

13 Christ. Panel icon by Kontoglou. 88

14 Christ in Benediction. Painting by El Greco. 89

15 Saint John the Baptist, Church of the Protaton. Panel icon. 90

16 Saint John the Baptist. Painting by El Greco. 91

17 The Baptism of Christ, Monastery of Iviron, Mount Athos. Miniature. 92

18 The Baptism of Christ. Painting by El Greco. 93

Illustrations

19 Excerpt from a composition by Petros the Peloponnesian in the reformed Byzantine notation.   106

20 Transcription of the excerpt into Western musical notation.   107

CHAPTER ONE

PHILOSOPHY

In his preface to Basil Tatakis' *La Philosophie byzantine,* which was first published in 1949 as a supplement to Volume I of *Histoire de la philosophie* by Emile Brehier, the latter observes: "No philosopher has attempted until now to study Byzantine philosophy in its entirety. At most it has been viewed as an aberrant branch of Western philosophy, as something reserved from the riches of Hellenism which, at the requisite moment, beginning with the 13th and above all with the 15th century, would serve to nourish Western thought."[1] One has only to glance at the various histories of philosophy, both general and those concerned with the Medieval period, in order to realize the correctness of Brehier's remark. Tatakis, who is professor of philosophy at the University of Thessaloniki, is the first to have attempted a comprehensive history of the philosophy of the Byzantine Empire. But even his work, although far more comprehensive than anything yet published on Byzantine philosophy, does not treat the whole of this subject. Tatakis' account starts from the sixth century. But the Byzantine Empire may be said to have begun in 330 A.D., when Constantine the Great, the first Christian Emperor, became the sole ruler of the Greco-Roman world and made the Greek city of Byzantium the capital of his empire; and the characteristic Byzantine way of philosophizing can be seen in writings of that time, and in much earlier ones, which appeared in the Hellenic East.

Brehier also remarks on the *autonomy* of Byzantine philosophy. "In Byzantium," he says, "there was a completely autonomous movement of ideas."[2] And Tatakis often calls attention to this fact in his book. Earlier writers had generally seen in Byzantine philosophical thought mere echoes of Plato and Aristotle. "This manner of seeing Christian thought, both in the East and in the

West, as an oscillation between Aristotelianism and Platonism, teaches us very little," says Tatakis. "One becomes content with this classification, one sees the form of thought, a little of its direction, and one concerns himself but little with its substantial content, with its foundation, with Christian truth, which it bears within itself."[3]

The autonomy of Byzantine philosophy is seen in the following two facts: (a) In the fact that the foundation of Byzantine philosophy is neither Platonic nor Aristotelian, but *Christian*: is *revelation;* and hence the elements borrowed from Platonism and Aristotelianism and the rest of ancient Greek philosophy acquire in Byzantine thought a *new* significance, being incorporated into Christianity in an *organic* manner.[4] (b) In the fact that thought develops in the Hellenic Christian East *independently* of the thought of the *Latin West.* Thus Brehier observes that "in the realm of Christianity, the thought of the Greek Fathers is very distinct in spirit from that of the Latin Fathers, which came after it."[5] And Tatakis remarks that "the work of the Western Fathers was almost totally ignored by the Byzantines."[6]

Despite the fact that both Brehier in the preface and Tatakis in his opening pages and elsewhere in *La Philosophie byzantine* speak of the *autonomy* of Byzantine philosophy, in treating individual authors Tatakis tends to envisage Byzantine philosophic thought too much in terms of the elements which it borrowed from ancient Greek philosophy, or of its similarities to the latter, and with reference to the ways in which it anticipated Western Renaissance thought. He is right, to be sure, in calling attention to the continuity between ancient Greek philosophy and Byzantine thought in certain formal respects, just as those who have studied Byzantine art have often called attention to a certain continuity that exists between the art of the ancient Greeks and the art of the Byzantines. But his preoccupation with this aspect of Byzantine thought, which is of secondary importance, often results in a shift of the emphasis away from what is deepest and most important in Byzantine philosophy.

Closely connected with this tendency in Tatakis' treatment of Byzantine philosophy is his failure to distinguish the *different senses* in which the term *philosophy* is used by the Byzantines and to treat Byzantine philosophy with close reference to these different senses. With few exceptions, the figures discussed in *La Philosophie byzantine* cannot be called philosophers, if we take the term philosopher in the sense in which it is used in Europe and America. Tatakis himself occasionally notes that the writer he is discussing is *not* really a "philosopher," but a "theologian." Yet he does not account for the fact that he has included such a writer in a book which purports to deal with *philosophy*. Thus, in speaking of St. John Damascene, to whom he devotes a whole chapter, he observes that "properly speaking," St. John "is neither a philosopher nor a savant, but a *theologian*."[7] Also, in the chapter in which he discusses the *hesychast* or mystical teaching of St. Gregory the Sinaite, St. Gregory Palamas and Nicholas Cavasilas, and the views of their opponents, such as Barlaam and Akindynos, Tatakis observes that "the hesychast quarrel began and ended as a clearly *theological* quarrel."[8] If then we take the term philosophy in its current sense, Tatakis' book can more appropriately be called a work on *theology* than one on philosophy. The term philosophy in its title could only be justified if, following the Byzantines, we were to broaden it to include theology. But this would require a good deal of explanation, which is not to be found in *La Philosophie byzantine*.

The writers with whom that book deals are for the most part known as Greek Church Fathers. Now the Greek Fathers distinguish two major, very different kinds of "philosophy." One of these they call "external" (*exōterikē, exō, thyrathen*) or "secular" (*kata kosmon*); the other, "internal" (*esōterikē, esō*) or "spiritual" (*pneumatikē*). *External* philosophy comprises for them ancient Greek philosophy and the pagan philosophy of the early Christian centuries. The term *internal* philosophy has a number of denotations. It is used to denote: (a) *Christian teaching* as a body of doctrines, ideas, and methods transmitted orally or in writing; (b) *lived* Christian teaching in general; (c) some *special form of spiritual striving,* especially inner quiet and inner attention; (d) *love of God;* (e) the *monastic life and principles.* The term philosophy is frequently used by the Fathers without a qualifying word to denote external philosophy, or some one of the various senses of internal philosophy. In what sense it is used in a particular instance has to be inferred from the context. In the West internal philosophy in sense (a) was and is denoted by the terms *dogmatic* and *revealed theology*. Hence in treating Byzantine philosophy one would have to deal not only with philosophy in the current sense of the term, but also with such theology and with some other topics besides.

There are only two significant Byzantine philosophers who can be characterized as secular: John Italos, "the Italian," and George Gemistos or Pletho. Italos (fl. 11th century)—who as a young man left southern Italy and went to Constantinople, where he succeeded Michael Psellos as professor of philosophy at the university—made philosophy an activity entirely independent of Christian revelation. He adopted an inflexible rationalistic approach and fell into heresies. He taught the preexistence of the soul and reincarnation, and rejected the doctrine of eternal hell and the veneration of holy icons. This resulted in the condemnation of his teaching by the Orthodox Church. Italos escaped anathematization by publicly declaring repentance and giving up his heretical views. He remained a Christian. But Pletho (*c.* 1355-1452)—a scholar and philosopher who was born and educated in Constantinople and later settled at Mystra—abandoned Christianity and in fact became anti-Christian. He condemned Christianity as decadent thought, went back to pre-Christian religion and philosophy—to Zoroaster, Plato, Aristotle, and the Stoics—and formulated the principles of a Utopian State. The primary concern of Pletho was to reform the Byzantine State socially and administratively, so as to enable it to withstand the external enemies and inner forces that were threatening its very existence toward the middle of the fifteenth century. Tatakis aptly remarks that "before appearing as a metaphysician, Pletho was a sociologist."[9] And he calls Pletho "a precursor and ancestor of the socialists and of many modern conceptions: nationalization of the army, intensification of national commerce, protection and encouragement of national production, war on imported luxuries, etc."[10]

For the Greek Fathers, Christianity is the truest and highest philosophy (*philosophia*), because it was revealed by Christ, Who is God's Wisdom (*Sophia*). Perhaps the first who used the term philosophy in this sense was Justin Martyr the Philosopher (*c.* 100-164), the most important of the Apologists. Justin speaks of Christian teaching as the "divine philosophy" (*philosophia theia*),[11] "the only safe and profitable philosophy,"[12] which is "greater than all human teaching."[13] It is divine and surpasses all human wisdom because it is "inspired by the Divine Wisdom or Logos,"[14] i.e. Christ. Consistently with his conception of Christianity as the *divine philosophy,* Justin continued to wear the philosopher's cloak after he became a Christian. He was not unique in this respect. St. Jerome tells us of one of the earliest Apologists, Aristides of Athens (fl. 140), that he was a philosopher who retained his philosopher's garb after his conversion to Christianity.[15] And Eusebios mentions three other Christians who wore the philosopher's garb: Heraclas, Aidesios, and Porphyrios. Heraclas (*c.* 180-247), a student of Ammonios Saccas, founder of Neo-Platonism, was converted to Christianity by Origen and assisted the latter at the Catechetical School of Alexandria. He continued to wear the philosopher's cloak after his ordination to presbyter.[16] Aidesios and Porphyrios were martyrs.[17]

Next to Justin, Clement of Alexandria (*c.* 150-*c.* 215) is a very notable Christian thinker who refers to Christian teaching as revealed philosophy. In his *Stromateis,* he says: "What we propose as our subject is not the discipline which obtains in each sect [of philosophy], but that which is really philosophy, strictly systematic Widsom, which furnishes acquaintance with the things which pertain to life. And we define Wisdom to be certain knowledge, being a sure and irrefragable apprehension of things divine and human, comprehending the present, past and future, which the Lord has taught us, both by His advent and by the prophets. And it is irrefragable by reason, inasmuch as it has been revealed. And so it is wholly true according to [God's] intention, as being known through the Son."[18]

Similarly, St. Nilos the Ascetic (fl. 440), a pupil of St. John Chrysostom, says: "Many of the Greeks and not a few of the Jews undertook to philosophize; but only Christ's disciples strove after the true wisdom, for they alone had Wisdom itself as their teacher, actually showing them the conduct proper for such a pursuit."[19]

Subsequent Greek Fathers, during the entire Byzantine period, continue to speak of Christianity in this manner, referring to it by such terms as "the true philosophy," "philosophy according to Christ," "heavenly philosophy," "spiritual philosophy," "divine philosophy," "sacred philosophy," "philosophy from Above," and "wisdom from Above."

It should be noted that while in the West the term "revealed theology" has been used to denote the greater part of what the Greek Fathers call "internal philosophy," in Byzantium the word theology was not used in this sense. The Byzantines employed the word theology in its strict, etymological sense, to refer only to works dealing with God.[20] It is consistently with this usage that Gregory Nazianzen (c. 329-c. 390) has been named "the Theologian." Thus A. J. Mason remarks: "It is in his lucid expositions of the doctrine of the Trinity that Gregory chiefly excels. By these it was that he won the title of 'the Theologian.' In simple and reverent language, without presumptuous over-definition, he enunciates the traditional belief, as championed by Athanasius, in a way which became the law of the future theologians."[21] Significantly, the Byzantines have given the title of "the theologian" to only two other writers: St. John the Gospel-writer, who speaks of the Divine "Word" or *Logos,* and Symeon the New Theologian (949-1022), the greatest Byzantine mystic, who authored a sublime poem, unique in the Hellenic East, in which he speaks of God and of the phases and conditions of mystical union with Him.[22] Restricting the denotation of the term theology to its etymological meaning, the Byzantines used the word *philosophy* as a generic term to refer to the whole of Christian teaching. In speaking of Christian ethics, they employ the term *ethical philosophy,* or simply philosophy; in speaking of that part of Christian teaching that pertains to the physical world, they employ the term *natural philosophy;* while in speaking of that part of Christian teaching that pertains to God they use the term *theological philosophy* or simply *theology.*

The denotation of the term philosophy to *lived* or *applied*

Christian teaching goes back to the early Fathers, such as Gregory
Nazianzen and John Chrysostom. It comes out with great clarity
and emphasis in the following passage of Nilos the Ascetic:
"Philosophy is a state of character (*ēthōn katastasis*) associated
with true belief regarding real being. This both the Jews and the
Greeks lacked, because they did not have the Wisdom that came
from heaven, and philosophized without Christ, Who alone exhibited the true philosophy both by deed and by word. For he
was the first one Who through His life opened its path, having
displayed a pure life and always kept His soul above the passions
of the body."[23] Similarly, Gregory the Sinaite (died 1360) remarks
that he is a true philosopher who *both knows and practices* the
Christian teaching; he "who has not only learned (*mathōn*) things
divine, but has experienced (*pathōn*) them. . . ."[24] And Gregory's
contemporary Nicholas Cavasilas (died 1371) says: "Through meekness, control of anger, not being vexed at those who offended Him,
and in many other ways the Savior introduced the true philosophy
into the world. He set forth far more and greater examples than
anyone else through what He did and what He patiently suffered."[25]

Occasionally, as we have noted, the word philosophy is employed to refer to such *spiritual practices* as inner quiet and inner
attention. These occupy a very important place in Eastern Orthodox
monasticism. However, they are not intended exclusively for the
use of monks. Through these practices one seeks to achieve purification (*katharsis*) of the soul and thereby illumination and union
with God. The use of the word philosophy in connection with
inner quiet (*hēsychia*) is found in the *Ladder* of St. John Climacos
(?579-?649) and other ascetic-mystical works. In this book, which
is one of the most remarkable Byzantine manuals on the spiritual
life, St. John describes the way to the highest spiritual attainments
through thirty steps. The twenty-seventh step is that of *hēsychia*,
"quiet" or "stillness." In discussing this step, he says at one point:
"Those who are thoroughly trained in secular philosophy are rare;
but I assert that those who understand the philosophy of true quiet
according to God are still rarer."[26] Mental quiet is "the putting
aside of thoughts and the rejection of even reasonable cares."[27]
Also it is "continuous worship and waiting upon God."[28]

Hesychios (died *c.* 433), who wrote an important discourse on *inner attention* or *inner wakefulness* (*nēpsis*), speaks of this practice as philosophy. It is, he says, "and is called intellectual or practical philosophy of the mind."[29] Again, he remarks: "If you wish to be truly good and gentle, and always united with God ... cultivate with all your power the virtue of attention, which is the guarding and watching of the mind, conducive to sweet quiet of the heart — a blessed state of the soul, free of fantasies. ... This is called mental philosophy (*noētē philosophia*)."[30] And the fourteenth century mystics Callistos Xanthopoulos and Ignatios Xanthopoulos say: "This is philosophy: that one be ever watchfully attentive even in the smallest things that befall him. A person who does this lays up for himself great treasures of inner rest. He does not fall asleep spiritually, lest anything adverse might befall him. He cuts off the causes in advance, suffers a little in small things and thereby banishes great suffering."[31]

Among those who speak of the *love of God* as philosophy are John Damascene and Gregory the Sinaite. In *The Fount of Knowledge,* the Damascene (*c.* 675-*c.* 749) gives six definitions of philosophy, the last of which is this: "Philosophy is love of wisdom. But the true wisdom is God. Therefore, the love of God — this is the true philosophy."[32] And St. Gregory says: "He is a divine philosopher who through practice and contemplation has become united directly with God, and has become and is said to be a lover of Him, inasmuch as he has loved the first and creative and true Wisdom more than every other love and wisdom and knowledge."[33]

The *ascetic, monastic life* has been regarded by the Byzantines as the highest, perfect form of the Christian life, "above nature and beyond common human living, ... devoted to the service of God alone in its wealth of heavenly love."[34] The term philosophy is often used by the Greek Fathers to denote this life and its principles.[35] Thus, in speaking of the monastic or eremitical life (*erēmikos bios*), Gregory Nazianzen says: "Our philosophy is humble in appearance, but sublime in its hidden essence, and leads to God."[36] Again he says: "As philosophy [the monastic life] is the greatest, so it is the most difficult of vocations, which can be undertaken by but few, and only by those who have been called forth by the

Divine magnanimity, which gives its hand to those who are honored by its preference."[37]

While extolling internal or spiritual philosophy, in the various senses which I have indicated, and placing it far above external philosophy, the Greek Fathers did not, in general, view the latter as of no value to the Christian. Most of those who undertook to defend the Christian Faith against attacks by non-Christian thinkers, to commend it to the cultured, to formulate Christian dogmas, or to incite Christian youth to virtue — *saw the value of a selective use* of external philosophy. Those, on the other hand, who lived in complete seclusion and confined themselves to striving for spiritual perfection and union with God, and addressed themselves exclusively to persons who aspired to embrace this way of life, regarded such knowledge as unnecessary for the attainment of their goal and the study of it as an impediment, insofar as it diverted the mind from prayer and contemplation.

In admitting a relative value to certain elements in Greek philosophy and an absolute value to revealed Christian teaching, the early Fathers of the East justified and initiated a *Christian eclecticism* that has continued in Greece down to the present day. This justification found classical expression in the *Stromateis* of Clement of Alexandria and in St. Basil's *Address to Young Men on How to Benefit by Greek Literature.*

Secular philosophy, asserts Clement, should not be regarded as evil. "Before the advent of the Lord, it was necessary to the Greeks for righteousness. And now it becomes conducive to piety, being a kind of preparatory training (*propaideia*) to those who attain to faith through demonstration."[38] It "was a schoolmaster to bring the Hellenic mind, as the Law the Hebrews, to Christ,"[39] and is "a stepping stone to the philosophy which is according to Christ."[40]

Truth, holds Clement, is not to be found in some one school of external philosophy alone. All the sects of philosophy, except those that are utterly senseless, possess fragments of eternal truth, some more and others less. "The way of truth," he remarks, "is one; but into it, as into a perennial river, streams flow from all sides."[41] Hence the Christian should seek to profit by all sects of philosophy. By "philosophy," says Clement, "I do not mean the Stoic, or the Platonic, or the Epicurean, or the Aristotelian, but whatever has been well said by each of those sects which teach righteousness along with knowledge pervaded by piety. This *eclectic whole* I call philosophy."[42] The discovery and assimilation of such truths exercises the mind and elicits the love of virtue.

In order to safeguard this position, Clement answers those who believe that philosophy is condemned in the Scriptures. They quote the Scriptural statements: "I will destroy the wisdom of the wise" (Isaiah 29: 14; 1 Cor. 1: 19); and: "The wisdom of this world is foolishness with God;" and again: "The Lord knoweth the thoughts of the wise, that they are vain" (1 Cor. 3: 19-20). Clement replies that these statements have reference to the sophists, "who devote their attention to empty words."[43] They also cite Paul's warning: "Beware lest any man spoil you through philosophy and vain deceit, after the tradition of men, after the rudiments of this world, and not after Christ" (Col. 2: 8). Clement's answer is that here the Apostle refers to those who have advanced from secular to spiritual philosophy, and warns them not to retrogress, not to substitute secular philosophy for Christianity, such philosophy "being most rudimentary" compared with Christianity, and only "a preparatory training for the truth."[44] Elsewhere in the *Stromateis* Clement interprets the passage of Paul just quoted as having reference to atheism, deism, and hedonism. The Apostle, he remarks, brands "not all philosophy, but the Epicurean, which abolishes Providence and deifies pleasure, and whatever other philosophy honors the elements, but places not over them the efficient cause, nor apprehends the Creator."[45]

As a Christian educator — he succeeded Pantainos as head of the Catechetical School at Alexandria — Clement is particularly interested in the value of Greek philosophy for catechumens. The catechist, he says, should be acquainted with this philosophy and should make judicious use of it in his classes, thereby helping the catechumens to a better understanding and appreciation of the true philosophy, Christian religion. "He who culls what is useful for the advantage of the catechumens, especially when they are Greeks, ... must collect as many aids as possible for his hearers. But he must by no means linger over these studies, except solely for the advantage accruing from them; so that when they have grasped and obtained this, he may be able to take his departure home to the true philosophy, which is a strong cable for the soul, providing security from everything."[46]

Basil's (?330-379) teaching on this subject is essentially the same as that of Clement, except that he links it quite explicitly with eschatology, the doctrine of the last things. In his *Address to Young Men on How to Benefit by Greek Literature,* directing himself to young Christians "who go to school every day," Basil stresses the otherworldly orientation of Christianity, which views the present life in relation to life after death. "We place our hopes upon the things which are beyond, and in preparation for the life eternal do all things that we do. Accordingly, whatever helps us towards this we say that we must love and follow after with all our might, but those things which have no bearing upon it should be held as naught."[47] Basil envisages Greek philosophical and other writings with this as a basic premise, and asserts that they are useful to Christian youth. Their value lies in the fact that they *prepare* the mind for the understanding of the Holy Scriptures, which lead to salvation. "Into the life eternal the Holy Scriptures lead us, which teach us through divine words. But so long as our immaturity forbids our understanding their deep thought, we exercise our spiritual perceptions upon secular writings which are not altogether different, and in which we perceive the truth as it were in shadows and mirrors."[48] Like the prisoners in the Cave described by Plato in the *Republic,* we must work our way to the apprehension of higher truth by stages. "Consequently we must be conversant with poets, with historians, with orators, indeed with all men who may further our soul's salvation."[49] We must "husband resources, leaving no stone unturned, as the proverb has it, whence we might derive any aid"[50] for the attainment of this goal.

Viewing human life under the aspect of eternity, we become cognizant of the fact that "virtue is the only possession that is sure, and that remains with us whether living or dead."[51] And "since we must needs attain to the life to come through virtue, our attention is to be chiefly fastened upon those many passages from the poets, from the historians, and especially from the philosophers, in which virtue itself is praised."[52] For "one who has been instructed in the pagan examples will no longer hold the Christian precepts impracticable."[53] Therefore, in reading the writings of secular authors, says Basil, we must *select* from them whatever is *true, incites to virtue and dissuades from vice.* The rest we must ignore. "We shall receive gladly those passages in which they praise virtue or condemn vice.... Altogether after the manner of bees must we use these writings, for the bees do not visit all the flowers without discrimination nor indeed do they carry away entire those upon which they light, but rather, having taken so much as is adapted to their needs, they let the rest go. So we, if wise, shall take from heathen books whatever befits us and is allied to the truth, and shall pass over the rest."[54]

Like Clement, Basil does not believe that such use of external learning is at all opposed by Scripture. Indeed, he points out examples of such use in the Old Testament. "Moses, whose name is a synonym for wisdom, severely trained his mind in the learning of the Egyptians.... Similarly, in later days, the wise Daniel is said to have studied the lore of the Chaldaeans while in Babylon, and after that to have taken up the sacred teachings."[55]

The standpoint of Clement reappears in the works of many subsequent Fathers. Thus, John Damascene, writing four centuries after Basil, makes the following remarks: "All Scripture" — the Old and the New Testaments — "is given by inspiration of God and is also assuredly profitable. Wherefore to search the Scriptures is a work most fair and most profitable for our souls.... In these we find both exhortation to every virtue and dissuasion from every vice. . . . Here let us luxuriate, let us revel insatiate; for the Scriptures possess inexhaustible grace. But if we are able to pluck anything profitable from outside sources, there is nothing to forbid that. Let us become tried money-dealers, heaping up the true and pure gold and discarding the spurious. Let us keep the fairest sayings, but let us throw to the dogs absurd gods and strange myths."[56] And Nicholas Cavasilas, who lived six centuries after the Damascene, says: "The Law became our instructor in Christ Jesus, and all the philosophy of men and every labor are introductions to, and preparations for, the true righteousness."[57]

The Christian eclecticism advocated by the Greek Fathers assigns a relative, conditional value to external philosophy, and implies the existence and conscious possession and use of an absolute system of truths, which makes it possible for the Christian to appropriate for himself what is true and valuable in external philosophy and pass over the rest. Apart from such a body of absolute, certain truths, one is left in a maze of conflicting human doctrines and opinions. The Fathers find this system of truths, this internal philosophy, in the Old and the New Testaments and in oral Sacred Tradition. These truths are not products of the fallen human mind, but have been revealed by God. As such, they constitute the supreme criterion for the selection and appropriation of elements from external philosophy.

Of all the ancient Greek philosophers, it was firstly in Plato and secondly in Aristotle that the Byzantines found elements that could be assimilated into Christian teaching. Among the most important ones that they adopted from Plato are the following: (a) the division of reality into the realm of intelligible things or true being and the realm of sensible things or phenomena; (b) the division of the human soul into three parts or faculties: the rational, the spirited, and the appetitive; (c) the view that the rational faculty is the highest part of the soul; (d) the doctrine of the four main virtues: wisdom, courage, temperance, and justice; (e) the doctrine of the unity of the virtues and the unity of the vices; (f) the view that knowledge is the primary condition of virtue and ignorance is the chief cause of vice. The most noteworthy elements they took over from Aristotle are: (a) the categories: substance, quantity, quality, relation, time, place, etc.; (b) the distinction between matter and form; (c) the view that virtue and vice are settled dispositions of the soul, or habits (*hexeis*); (d) the doctrine that moral virtue is a mean between two extremes, one of excess and the other of deficiency, both of which are vices. These elements began entering into the fabric of Greek Patristic thought from the early Christian centuries, especially with Athanasios, Basil, Gregory of Nyssa and Gregory Nazianzen, and recur in the writings of the Greek Fathers throughout the Byzantine period.

In being assimilated into Byzantine thought, they underwent significant modifications. A new meaning was infused into them, they were spiritualized. Thus, Plato says that reason should rule the two irrational powers of the soul, the spirited and the appetitive, according to wisdom. The wisdom that Plato presents is human wisdom, is the wisdom that is acquired through the exercise of man's reason. But the Byzantines tell us that reason should rule above all in accordance with another, higher wisdom, the revealed Law of God. Also, they stress two functions of the rational faculty which Plato seldom touches: inner attention and prayer. For the Byzantines these two functions become the most important ones, especially in the monastic life. In connection with the spirited part, they tell us that it should be directed not only to the control of the appetitive, but also against evil spirits, in accordance with St. Paul's remark: "For we wrestle not against flesh and blood, but against principalities, against powers, against the rulers of the darkness of this world, against spiritual wickedness in celestial places."[58] With regard to the appetitive part of the soul, they teach not merely that it should be restrained by reason and the spirited faculty, but also that it should be directed towards God. The four general virtues , too, are seen in a new context. They are viewed, for instance, as preconditions of the higher Christian virtues of faith, hope, and love. While seeing, like Plato, a close relationship between knowledge and virtue on the one hand, and ignorance and vice on the other, the Byzantines expand the term knowledge to include faith and the knowledge that comes from Divine illumination; and similarly they broaden the term ignorance to include unbelief and the lack of spiritual knowledge.

In accepting Aristotle's distinction between form and matter, the Byzantines do not accept his view that the human soul is the *form* (*eidos*) of the body. For them the soul is an immaterial *substance* (*ousia*). Nor do they accept his teaching that matter is beginningless, uncreated. Matter is *not* coeternal with God, but was created by God out of nothing. Also, while accepting Aristotle's doctrine that virtue is a mean, they emphatically disagree with Aristotle that jesting (*eutrapelia*) is a moral virtue, being a mean between buffoonery and boorishness. For them it is a vice

that relaxes·the tone of the soul. And they exalt complete continence, which in Aristotle's ethics is a form of the vice of "insensibility" (*anaisthēsia*).

The term *apatheia*, "passionlessness," appears frequently in the
writings of the Greek Fathers. It is the most notable one they took
over from the Stoic philosophers. But it acquires a meaning significantly different from that which it has in Stoicism. For the
Stoics it means the absence of emotions, whereas for the Byzantines it
means the absence not of all emotions, but only of wrong emotions,
such as malice and the attachment to material things and carnal
pleasures. More widely, *apatheia* means freedom from all vice and
sin. Far from involving for the Byzantines the absence of all
emotion, "passionlessness" is associated with the manifestation of
the highest emotion, that of spiritual love. It is significant that
in St. John Climacos' ladder of spiritual ascent, the 29th step is
Passionlessness, while the next one, the last, is Faith, Hope, and
Love.

Enough has been said to make clear the distinct senses in which
the term philosophy was used by the Greek Fathers, and also to
give some idea of the content and motivation of their philosophizing. All the senses in which the term is used are linked together
by the etymology of the word, which is "love (*philia*) of wisdom
(*sophia*)." Philosophy for them is the love of wisdom, both Divine
and human. It is love of *Divine* wisdom both in that it is the love
of Christ, Who is the Divine Logos or Wisdom, and in that it is the
love of the teaching that Christ revealed to mankind through deed
and word. It is love of *human* wisdom insofar as this wisdom is true
and conducive to virtue, being in accord with Divine wisdom.

The mainspring of the philosophizing of the Greek Fathers
is *existential*. Their aim is the salvation of man, of the individual,
the person. Characteristic of the Byzantine philosophic mind are
the remarks of Basil the Great that were quoted earlier: "We place
our hopes upon the things which are beyond, and in preparation
for the life eternal do all things that we do. Accordingly, whatever
helps us towards this we say that we must love and follow after with
all our might, but those things which have no bearing upon it should
be held as naught." Also characteristic is the following passage from

Symeon the New Theologian: "The faith which one has in Christ,
our true God, gives birth to desire for true blessings and to fear
of torments. Desire for real blessings and fear of torments lead
to a strict observance of the commandments. And the strict observance of the commandments teaches men their own weakness.
The realization of our actual weakness gives birth to memory of
death. He who has acquired memory of death as a companion will
seek with painful efforts to learn what awaits him after his departure from this life."[59]

True faith leads to a virtuous life; this, to higher spiritual
development; and this, in turn, to union with God or *theosis,*
"deification," and thereby to salvation. The Father traditionally
known as Dionysios the Areopagite asserts that "Salvation is not
possible otherwise than through *theosis;* and *theosis* is the attainment of likeness to God and union with Him."[60] It is usually held
today that this writer was in his prime towards the end of the fifth
century of the Christian Era. But the view just quoted is to be
found in the writings of earlier Church Fathers, such as St. Macarios
the Great, who lived in the fourth century. Macarios says: "No
soul which has not received God within herself now, and found rest
in Him, has an inheritance in the kingdom of heaven with the
saints, nor can she enter the heavenly city."[61] The idea recurs in
the works of subsequent writers. Symeon the New Theologian, for
instance, says in his remarkable mystical poem:

> "They alone are saved, He has said, who have participated
> In His Divinity, as He the Creator of all things
> Has participated in our nature.
> Hearken, He is called the Savior for this reason,
> Because He gives salvation to all with whom He unites Himself.
> Now salvation is deliverance from all evils,
> And the eternal finding in Him of all blessings."[62]

In its union with God the soul is not absorbed into Him, as
it is according to pantheistic mysticism. It retains its distinctness
and self-consciousness. Indeed, its individuality is not only retained
but enhanced. Niketas Stethatos (fl. 1030), the most outstanding

disciple of Symeon, observes that the Divine light in the soul integrates it, and the soul becomes one instead of remaining many othernesses. "And this," he says, "is the restoration (*apokatastasis*) of the soul and our renewal into something superior."[63]

CHAPTER TWO

THE WAY TO KNOWLEDGE

In their attempts to arrive at sound philosophical knowledge, most modern philosophers have adopted either the method of rationalism or that of empiricism. A smaller number have adopted the method of pragmatism, and a still smaller one that of intuitionism. Although these methods differ significantly, as pursued by modern philosophers they all rest on certain common presuppositions that are more important than their differences. These presuppositions are (a) that philosophical knowledge is to be pursued autonomously, independently of religious faith, and (b) that the philosopher can attain this knowledge by simply applying in as diligent a manner as possible some one of these methods. Religious faith, far from being considered as a necessary condition for sound philosophizing, has been regarded as something irrelevant or a positive hindrance to the attainment of truth. The philosopher's moral character and inner being in general have been tacitly assumed to be quite irrelevant to the successful pursuit of knowledge.

The approach of the Byzantines, with very few exceptions, involves a negation of both these presuppositions. Religious faith is for them an indispensable condition of sound philosophizing. The philosopher must begin with religious faith, if he is to avoid error and attain truth. Also, one's moral and spiritual state — whether one is courageous or cowardly, continent or incontinent, just or unjust, calm or irritable, humble or proud, disposed to love or to hate, and so on — is viewed by them as quite relevant to the pursuit of philosophical knowledge.

Underlying the approach of most modern philosophers has been a tacit or explicit optimism regarding man. They have either ignored or rejected the doctrine of the Fall. The Byzantines, however, take the doctrine of the Fall seriously, and chart their path to knowledge with close reference to it. Man is in a fallen state. He is not what he ought to be, and this applies to all his faculties. Thus, Symeon the New Theologian says: "From the time of the transgression of Adam all the natural powers of human nature have been corrupted: intuitive reason, discursive reason, the faculty of opinion, imagination, and sensation.... And this is why man is able to think, but he cannot think soundly. He is able to desire, but he desires foolishly. He is able to be angry, but becomes angry unreasonably. As a result, both what he apprehends by his reason, and what he thinks and opines, as well as what he imagines and feels and senses are distorted and faulty."[1] The Fall was a turning away from God, a separation from God and His vivifying and illuminating grace. Accepting man's fallen state as a fact, the Byzantines concern themselves with the problem of how man's nature can be restored to its pristine, natural state, how man's faculties can be made to function normally. The path which leads to this state is seen to be that of virtue. Through virtue, passionlessness or inner purity is achieved; through purity man gains consciousness of the knowledge with which God has endowed his soul and attains union with God; and through union with God he rises to still higher knowledge.

A great deal is said by the Greek Fathers about how the vices, passions, and overt sins darken the soul and make impossible the perception of objective truth, of things as they really are. Thus, Mark the Ascetic (fl. 430) says: "The mind is blinded by these three passions: avarice, vanity, pleasure.... It is through these and nothing else that knowledge and faith, these companions of our nature, have been blunted."[2] Similarly, John Climacos remarks: "Higher perception is an attribute of the soul; but sin buffets perception."[3]

Through the cultivation of what the Byzantines call virtue, which includes not only the four cardinal virtues of Plato, the Christian virtues of faith, hope, love, etc., but also practices such as inner attention and prayer, one moves from the darkness of ignorance and error to the light of knowledge and understanding. The upward movement begins with *faith*. "A mind which begins to philosophize about things divine," remarks St. Maximos the Confes-

sor (580-662), "begins with faith."[4] And Niketas Stethatos asserts
that "faith precedes all the virtues."[5] Real faith consists in the
voluntary assent of the soul to Christian teaching, to the word of
God, and living in accordance with this teaching. "The mark of
true believers," says Symeon the New Theologian, "is this, never
to transgress at all in anything the commandments of the Great
God and our Savior Jesus Christ."[6] Maximos the Confessor sums
up in one sentence how from faith one rises to illumination: "He
who believes, fears God; he who fears God becomes humble; he
who becomes humble becomes meek, acquiring a settled disposition
that is not disturbed by the movements of anger and desires that
are contrary to nature; he who is meek keeps the commandments
of God; he who keeps the commandments is purified; and he who
is purified is illumined. . . . "[7]

Humility is another exceedingly important virtue in one's striving for higher knowledge. Mark the Ascetic says: "I have seen
unlettered men who, having humbled themselves in deed, became
wiser than the wise."[8] Again he remarks: "One's knowledge is
true in proportion as it is confirmed by meekness, humility, and
love."[9] Similarly, Symeon the New Theologian observes: "If you
find yourself in a state of contrition and humility, know that you
have been illumined; and the humbler you become the more
you will be illumined."[10] And Hesychios tells us: "The way to
knowledge is through passionlessness and humility, without which
no one shall see the Lord."[11] Humility comes from self-knowledge.
In fact, Niketas Stethatos and other Byzantines explicitly identify
it with self-knowledge. Stethatos says: "Know thyself; this indeed
is true humility, which teaches us to be humble, which makes the
heart contrite. . . . If you have not yet come to know yourself, you
do not know what humility is either."[12] Humility is the state of
being keenly aware of one's faults, one's shortcomings. It is the
painful awareness of the chasm that exists between what we are
and what we ought to be, between our actual self and our ideal self.
From humility as self-knowledge or consciousness of oneself as one
really is one advances to a knowledge or consciousness of God.
Keenly aware of one's fallen state, one begins to strive more
arduously for spiritual perfection, for likeness to God and union

with Him.

From living faith comes humility; out of humility grows *love* of God and of our fellow men; and through this love we progress in knowledge. The intimate relationship between humility and love is stressed by Abba Isaiah, Symeon the New Theologian, Stethatos, and others. Isaiah (4th century) remarks that "conscious surrender of oneself to God and obedience to His commandments in humility bring love;"[13] while Symeon calls humility the "root of love."[14] Concerning the close relationship between love and knowledge we have the testimony of John Climacos, Abba Thalassios, Maximos the Confessor, and many others. Climacos asserts that "love bestows prophecy; . . . love is an abyss of illumination."[15] Thalassios (7th century) exhorts us: "Let us acquire faith in order to come to love, from which is born the illumination of knowledge."[16] Maximos calls love "the way to truth," and remarks: "The life of reason (*nous*) is the illumination of knowledge, and this is brought to birth by love of God; hence it has been rightly said that there is nothing greater than divine love."[17] Again he says: "He who has genuinely renounced worldly things, and sincerely serves his neighbor through love, is quickly freed from every passion and becomes a partaker of God's love and knowledge."[18]

Through faith, humility, love and the other virtues *passionlessness* or *purity* is attained. Passionlessness is freedom not only from all overt sin, but also from all vice and all bad or negative thoughts and feelings; and is achieved through a gradual and sustained process of purification effected by a life in accordance with God's commandments. It presupposes the attainment of all the virtues. Peter Damascene (fl. 775) quotes Christ's statement: "Blessed are the pure in heart, for they shall see God," and comments: "This means those who have achieved every virtue."[19] Passionlessness is sometimes characterized as the "resurrection of the soul," which precedes the resurrection of the body. The close connection between passionlessness and knowledge is frequently stressed by the Greek Fathers. Abba Philemon, who lived sometime before the ninth century, asserts, for instance, that "the more the mind is stripped of passions and purified, the more it becomes worthy of knowledge."[20] Similarly, Niketas Stethatos says: "The wisdom of God penetrates

and enters all those whom it finds in a state of purity."[21] And
Symeon of Thessaloniki (15th century) observes: "God grants His
divine light in proportion to our purity."[22]

In emphasizing the close relationship between passionlessness
or purity and the acquisition of knowledge, the Byzantines often
specify *what* one comes to know, or to know *better,* as a result of
passionlessness. Sometimes it is said to be reality in general. But
more often it is said to be a spiritual reality: the soul, angels, the
future life, the kingdom of heaven, God. Thus Abba Thalassios says:
"Just as spring stirs up plants to growth, so passionlessness awakens
the mind to a knowledge of things."[23] And later he remarks:
"When the Holy Spirit finds the mind stripped of passions, It
teaches it mystically about all the things hoped for."[24] Abba Philemon observes that "when one's mind reaches the limit of purity,
God reveals to him visions (*theōriai*) of the ministering spirits."[25]
And Maximos the Confessor remarks: "Cleanse your mind of
anger, malice, and bad thoughts, and then you will be able to know
the indwelling of God.... The Savior says: 'Blessed are the pure
in heart, for they shall see God.' They shall see him and the
treasures within Him when they have cleansed themselves through
love and self-control; and the more so the more they intensify the
purification."[26]

Inner purity results in the removal of the psychical barriers
that make our innate knowledge inaccessible to us, that keep it
buried in the unconscious. It also makes us receptive of Divine
grace, which opens our spiritual eyes and awakens the other spiritual
senses. The moral knowledge in conscience is an example of innate
knowledge that remains more or less unconscious. Conscience is
sometimes spoken of by the Greek Fathers as a "teacher"[27] or
"natural book."[28] It is a book which is easily read by those who are
accustomed to obey its counsels, but becomes more or less illegible
to those who tend to ignore it and trample upon it again and again,
following instead bad thoughts and desires. Then conscience becomes imbedded in the subconscious level of the soul. When the
soul is cleansed, when it attains a state of passionlessness, then
conscience is uncovered, is brought back to consciousness. The moral
laws which God has inscribed upon it become clear and distinct.[29]

The knowledge possessed by conscience, the knowledge of good and evil, is but a part of man's innate knowledge. Man is born with a vast treasure of knowledge pertaining to the whole created world and to God. This knowledge is termed "natural knowledge" (*physikē gnōsis*). Plato took cognizance of it and tried to account for it by means of the theory of the preexistence of the soul. The Greek Fathers reject the theory of preexistence and account for this knowledge by reference to the Scriptural teaching that man was created in the image and likeness of God. Within God are contained the reasons, ideas, or archetypes of all things. Hence God is said to be perfect Wisdom. Unlike Plato, who vacillated between placing the eternal ideas or archetypes in the Divine Mind and making them an independent metaphysical factor, the Byzantines definitely deny them independent existence and hold that they have their being within the mind of God. Now since man has been created in the image of God, he must reflect within himself God, and hence all these ideas.

St. Athanasios the Great and St. Gregory of Nyssa are among the first to have expressed this view. "The soul," remarks Athanasios (*c.* 298-373), "is made after the image and likeness of God, as divine Scripture shows, when it says in the person of God: 'Let us make man after our Image and likeness.' Whence also when it gets rid of all the filth of sin which covers it and retains only the likeness of the Image in its purity, then surely this latter being thoroughly brightened, the soul beholds as in a mirror the Image of the Father, even the Word (*Logos*), and by His means reaches the idea of the Father, Whose Image the Savior is."[30] Expressing this view more fully, Gregory of Nyssa (*c.* 331-396) writes: "God made human nature a participator of every good. For if the Deity is the fullness of goods, and man is His image, it follows that the likeness of the image to the archetype consists in its being, too, full of every good. Hence there is within us the idea of everything beautiful and also every virtue and all wisdom. . . ."[31] This view appears in the writings of later Fathers. Niketas Stethatos, for example, says: "Just as the Creator of all things, even before He created all things out of nonbeing, had the knowledge, the natures, and the reasons of all things within Himself, being the king of

eternity and the foreknower, so he made man, whom He created in
His image as the king of the created world, a possessor of the
reasons, natures, and knowledge of all things."[32]

This knowledge is called *natural,* because it exists in our nature
and is not a product of learning. It is also known by other names.
Speaking about this knowledge, Peter Damascene remarks that it
"is called by some 'good sense' (*phronēsis*), because the mind sees
things as they are in their nature. By others it is called 'insight'
(*diorasis*), because he who has it [at the level of consciousness]
knows part of the hidden mysteries, that is, the purpose of God
which is contained in the Divine Scriptures and in each creature. . . .
It is able to understand the reasons of sensible things and of intelligible things; and hence it is called 'contemplation' of beings,
that is, of creatures. This knowledge is called natural, and comes
[to consciousness] from purity of mind. . . . It preexisted in our
nature, but the passions darkened the mind, and it cannot see, unless,
as a result of moral virtue, God removes the passions."[33]

"Natural knowledge" (*physikē gnōsis*) should not be con-
founded with "knowledge according to nature" (*kata physin gnōsis*). The latter is not innate but acquired. It develops out of
natural knowledge through experience and reasoning. Natural
knowledge provides the foundations, the premises, the starting
points of such knowledge. Thus, Theodore of Edessa (fl. 660) says:
"We call 'knowledge according to nature' that part of knowledge
which the soul can acquire through inquiry and search, using the
sense-organs and natural faculties, concerning both the created
world and the Cause of the created world."[34]

In proportion as a man grows in passionlessness, his *natural
knowledge* rises to consciousness, and his *knowledge according to
nature* becomes sound, free of error. To the degree, on the other
hand, that he remains chained to the "passions" (*pathē*) — to bad
thoughts and feelings, to vice and sin — his natural knowledge
remains buried in the unconscious, and the knowledge which he
acquires through inquiry and search is *not according* to nature,
but *contrary* to nature (*para physin*), unsound, a mixture of truth
and error. Such knowledge is also referred to as "worldly" (*kata
kosmon*), the "world" being the passions, man's fallen state.

Natural knowledge and knowledge according to nature are distinguished from a higher kind of knowledge, which is *"above nature"* (*hyper physin*), "supernal" (*hyperphyēs*), "spiritual" (*pneumatikē*). This knowledge is a direct revelation of spiritual law, of the Divine will, of the hidden mysteries of the kingdom of heaven. It comes from the indwelling of Divine grace in those who have achieved purity. After describing knowledge according to nature, Theodore of Edessa says about supernal knowledge that it "is knowledge which comes to the mind independently of its method and is above its power. This knowledge comes only from God, whenever He finds the mind exceedingly cleansed of every material attachment and full of divine love."[35] Hesychios writes: "He who with all diligence keeps his heart pure shall have as his teacher and lawgiver Christ, mystically uttering His will to him. 'I will hear what the Lord God will utter within me,' says David (Ps. 85:8), indicating this."[36] Similarly, Maximos the Confessor remarks: "He who has brought the body into harmony with the soul through virtue . . . becomes, through purity of mind, an abode of the Logos."[37] Such a person is said to have risen to a state of illumination (*phōtismos*), of *theosis* or union with God, *theosis* being not only man's highest state of being, involving the complete turning of the will and the emotions towards God, but also his highest state of knowledge.

From what has been said about the Byzantine way to knowledge, it is evident that knowledge is sought by the Byzantines neither in the manner of the rationalists, nor in the manner of the empiricists, nor in that of the pragmatists. The Byzantines begin with religious faith, with the free acceptance of revelation. This, having the impress of Divine authority, is absolute. Faith for them is *not* "a leap in the dark," as it is for many moderns. Such a position could be used to justify the adoption of the most absurd and inhuman doctrines. The Byzantines assent inwardly to Christ's teaching because they find it consonant with their natural moral teacher, conscience, and with the rest of their "natural knowledge;" and consonant also — as we have noted in discussing Justin Martyr, Clement of Alexandria, Basil, and John Damascene —[38] with many things said by the ancient Greeks, especially the philosophers.

The Byzantines are closest to intuitionism. The knowledge possessed by conscience, our natural knowledge in general, and spiritual knowledge is unmediated, not a product of deductive or inductive reasoning. Where the Byzantines differ from modern intuitionism, such as that of Bergson, is in the account they give of the source of this knowledge, in the vast range it covers for them, and in the conditions they specify for its manifestation — the acceptance of revealed teaching and life in accordance with it. The range of modern intuitionism is relatively narrow, and its starting point is, in general, secular.

Discursive reason, sense-experience, and pragmatic tests do play a part in the Byzantines' quest for knowledge, but this part is a secondary one. In rationalism, it is discursive reason that plays the prominent role; in Byzantine intuitionism it is intuitive reason. And significantly, while for rationalism reason is a static faculty, which is present in its natural state in all men, for the Byzantines reason is in general present in a warped and unnatural state. Characteristic of these two standpoints are the following remarks made by Descartes, father of modern rationalism, and by Gregory the Sinaite, one of the great Byzantine mystics. Descartes writes in the opening part of his *Discourse on Method*: "The power of forming a good judgment and of distinguishing the true from the false, which is properly speaking what is called good sense or reason, is by nature equal in all men. . . . The diversity of our opinions does not proceed from some men being more rational than others, but solely from the fact that our thoughts pass through diverse channels and the same objects are not considered by all." Gregory, on the other hand, remarks: "It is impossible for one to be or become rational according to nature, as man originally was, before attaining purity and incorruption. . . . They alone are rational according to nature, who have achieved purity, namely, the saints. None who are wise in words possess pure reason, their rational faculty having been corrupted by the passions."[39]

The Byzantines do not deny the value of outer experience in the acquisition of knowledge. But whereas for empiricism it is primary, for them it is secondary. The physical senses are the sources neither of "natural knowledge" nor of "spiritual knowledge." For the Byzantines it is not outer but inner seeing and hearing that is important. They emphasize self-observation: the observing of one's thoughts and emotions, desires and habits; and self-perfection: the cultivation of what is good in oneself and the opposition of all that is bad. They especially stress listening attentively to the voice of conscience and following its promptings. It is in this manner that one advances in self-knowledge, and through self-knowledge to a knowledge of the whole of reality. "He who knows himself knows everything," remarks St. Antony the Great.[40] Similarly, Peter Damascene says: "To him who has come to know himself is given knowledge of all things."[41]

Pragmatic criteria are not used by the Byzantines to test their faith, to determine for instance whether they are right in believing that God and the soul exist, and whether the soul is immortal and the will free. What they test pragmatically, "by their fruits," are visions and extraordinary states, to determine whether these are authentic or spurious. That God and the soul exist, that the soul is immortal and the will free, and so on, are truths they never doubt. These constitute firm starting points of the Byzantines' quest for knowledge.

CHAPTER THREE

CONSCIENCE

Much of uncommon interest and value is said by the Byzantine or Greek Fathers concerning the important human faculty known as conscience. Their teaching on this subject is based on Holy Scripture and on their inner experience, a product of a life ordered in accordance with the word of God. What is said in Scripture is repeated by them, interpreted, illustrated, amplified. The later Fathers reiterate what was said by the earlier ones, confirm it, often elaborate it.

The terms which they use to denote conscience are *syneidēsis* and *syneidos*. The first of these terms occurs in the New Testament. Most of the New Testament references are in the Epistles of the Apostle Paul. In his Epistles conscience is distinguished from the rational faculty on the one hand and from the heart on the other. It is distinguished from reason when Paul remarks: "In the case of the defiled and the unbelieving, nothing is pure, both their mind and their conscience being defiled;"[1] and from the heart, when he says: "The end of the commandment is love out of a pure heart and of a good conscience."[2] Conscience is spoken of as being either good or evil, clear or defiled. It is clear when in all respects we live as we ought to; and defiled, when we act wrongly. An accompaniment of a clear conscience is joy: "Our rejoicing is this, the testimony of our conscience that we have behaved in the world, and still more towards you, with holiness and godly sincerity."[3] Paul also makes reference to conscience in the Acts of the Apostles. He speaks of following conscience in relation to God and to neighbor. "And herein do I exercise myself," he says, "to have always a conscience void of offense towards God and towards men."[4]

Significant statements about conscience are also made by the Apostles John and Peter. John speaks of the scribes and Pharisees as "being censured (*elenchomenoi*) by their conscience,"[5] while

Peter stresses the need of having a "good conscience towards God."[6]

The distinction of conscience from the other powers, which we noted in Paul, appears also in the writings of the Greek Fathers. Conscience is distinguished by the Fathers from the rational faculty, the will, the imagination, etc. They clearly do not take it to be something acquired, a mere product of social conditioning, as it is fashionable to regard conscience today, but view it as a distinct faculty or power (*dynamis*) implanted in the soul by God.

Conscience, they tell us, is a moral guide and judge, as well as an awakener of higher thoughts and feelings. In its operation as a *moral guide* it acts both negatively and positively. It tells us not only what is evil and hence to be avoided, but also what is good and hence to be done. Thus, Abba Dorotheos, one of the great ascetic-mystical Fathers, who was in his prime at the end of the sixth and the beginning of the seventh centuries, says in his *Diverse Edifying Teachings*: "When God created man, He implanted in him something divine, like a certain warm and luminous thought having a spark of reason, to illumine the mind and distinguish good from evil. This is called conscience, and is natural law."[7] The importance of conscience as a moral guide is stressed also by Maximos the Confessor, John Climacos, and others. Maximos says: "Do not dishonor your conscience, which always gives you excellent counsel. For it offers you divine and angelic advice."[8] Similarly, John Climacos tells us: "After God let us have our conscience as our aim and rule in everything."[9]

Intimately related to the activity of conscience as a moral guide is its operation as a *moral judge*. Conscience judges our acts as to rightness and wrongness. When we act rightly, it remains silent, whereas when we act wrongly it accuses us. In this role as a judge, conscience is impartial. The Fathers stress this impartiality. Thus John Chrysostom remarks: "Within conscience there are no flatterers, no wealth to corrupt the judge."[10] And John Climacos asserts: "He who has obtained the fear of the Lord has given up lying, having his conscience as an unbribable judge."[11]

The impartiality or objectivity of conscience is a result of the involuntary character of its activity, its independence of our will. When we act rightly, it was noted, conscience remains silent, unaccusing. A person who through pious living has acquired an unaccusing conscience is known as a saint. But there are instances where the absence of remorse of conscience, far from being a sign of a saintly life, is a result of depravity. John Climacos remarks: "Let us observe carefully whether our conscience has ceased to accuse us, not as a result of our purity, but because we are plunged in wickedness."[12] Thus, an unaccusing conscience is a sign that one is either a saint or a great sinner. Abba Thalassios puts the matter this way: "Those alone are not accused by their conscience who have either reached the summit of virtue or have sunk to the depths of vice."[13]

Accompanying the quiet of conscience that occurs in the saint are inner peace, hope, moral courage, fearlessness of death, higher knowledge, spiritual love and joy. The joy that comes from having a clear conscience is especially emphasized by the Byzantines. Thus Chrysostom remarks: "As for good spirits and joy, it is not greatness of power, not abundance of wealth, not pomp of authority, not strength of body, not sumptuousness of the table, not the adorning of dresses, nor any other of the things in man's reach that ordinarily produces them, but spiritual success and a good conscience alone. And he that has his conscience cleansed, even though he be clad in rags and struggling with famine, is of better spirits than they that live softly."[14] Epitomizing the Byzantine teaching on this point, Nicodemos the Aghiorite says: "To have an unaccusing conscience is indeed the pleasure of pleasures and the joy of joys."[15]

In the case of the extremely bad, the silence of conscience is the silence of a faculty that is no longer alive at the level of ordinary consciousness. Such quiet is the final result, not only of repeated wrong acts over a long period, but also of rationalizations or the calming of conscience by sham reasoning. Hesychios warns: "If a person deceives his conscience by sham arguments, he will fall asleep in the bitter death of forgetfulness."[16]

Preceding this state of complete absence of remorse is one in which, owing to the continual indwelling in us of bad thoughts and emotions, the voice of conscience becomes more and more faint and indistinct, its dictates progressively distorted and suppressed. Conscience is then said to be "impure" or "defiled."

Because conscience censures us for our wrong acts, inner as well as outer, it is sometimes characterized as the "accuser" (*antidikos*). "Conscience" says Abba Dorotheos, "is called the accuser, because it always opposes our evil volitions and censures us for not doing what we ought to do, and for doing what we ought not to do, and accuses us."[17] Dorotheos finds the idea of conscience as an accuser in the following statement of Jesus: "Agree with thine accuser quickly, while thou art in the way with him, lest at any time the accuser hand thee over to the judge, and the judge deliver thee to the guard, and thou be cast into prison."[18] "By 'in the way,' comments Dorotheos, "Jesus means 'while you are in this world,' as Basil the Great says."[19]

That conscience judges not only our *deeds* but also our *dispositions* is attested by Macarios the Great (300-390), when he says that conscience "censures those thoughts that assent to sin ... and reproves and directs the heart."[20]

The activity of conscience as an accuser is a very painful experience. Chrysostom remarks that "he who lives in wickedness experiences the torments of hell prior to hell, being stung by his conscience."[21] Again he says: "Nothing so weighs upon the soul and presses it down as consciousness of sin."[22] Similar statements occur in numerous Byzantine writings, including the hymnography of the Greek Orthodox Church. One of the hymns of the *Triōdion,* says in part: "Hence I have been censured, hence I the wretch have been condemned by my own conscience, than which nothing in the world is more violent."[23] In another of the liturgical books of the Greek Church, the *Paraklētikē* or the *Great Octōēchos,* we find the following hymn: "I shudder, as I think of your coming, O Master; for I have my judgment prior to the Judgment, my conscience within accusing me prior to the torments of hell."[24]

The experience of remorse should not lead to despair, but should only intensify a person's efforts to obey his conscience. "It is the property of angels not to fall," says John Climacos, "but it is the property of men to fall, and to rise again whenever this happens."[25]

Besides functioning as a moral guide and judge, conscience acts as an awakener. "A clear conscience," observes Abba Thalassios,

"arouses the soul."[26]   Other Fathers specify ways in which conscience
awakens us. Thus Macarios asserts that conscience "wakes up the
natural thoughts of which the heart is full."[27] He identifies "natural
thoughts" with the "pure thoughts" that the Lord created."[28]
Chrysostom says that conscience evokes humility: "Conscience,
turning the soul on itself, causes it to become humble."[29] And
Climacos mentions holy contrition (*katanyxis*) as an effect of active
conscience.[30] He characterizes contrition as "gladdening sorrow"
(*charmolypē*), because it "has gladness and sorrow interwoven
within it like honey in the comb."[31] Contrition in turn stirs up love
of God and neighbor. Thus Niketas Stethatos observes that "nothing rouses the soul to eros for God and love of man as humility,
contrition, and pure prayer."[32]

A defiled conscience has the opposite effects. It puts to sleep,
deadens man's higher functions. Chrysostom poignantly remarks:
"As in severe frost all the limbs are stiffened and dead, so truly
the soul shuddering in the winter of sins also performs none of its
proper functions, stiffened as it were by a frost as to conscience
For what cold is to the body, that an evil conscience is to the soul."[33]

In speaking of unaccusing conscience, we noted that it indicates
either a state of extreme purity, or one of depravity. The question
arises: What happens to conscience in the latter case? Is it de-
stroyed as a faculty? The answer is that conscience is never de-
stroyed, but only ceases to operate, as a result of being continually
ignored and suppressed. It becomes embedded in the subconscious
level of the psyche and ceases to manifest itself at the level of
consciousness, becomes dead at *this* level. One of the hymns in the
Paraklētikē says: "I present an uncorrected soul, my conscience
covered with the matter of my trespasses, my heart defiled, and my
thought tainted; I cry to Thee, O Lover-of-man, have compassion
on me in Thy mercy."[34] Abba Dorotheos similarly speaks of buried
conscience. He sees the first appearance of this state as an accompaniment of the Fall. The transgression of Adam and Eve greatly
affected conscience; it resulted in conscience's becoming covered up
and trampled on. Hence "we came to need written law, the holy
Prophets, and the very coming of our Savior Christ in order to
unbury and resurrect it, to vivify that buried spark."[35] The Christian

way of life, the keeping of the commandments of Christ, uncovered conscience, brought it back to consciousness. But we bury it again by transgressing the commandments. "When our conscience says, 'Do this,' and we despise this prompting, and again it tells us, and we do not do it, but continue trampling on conscience, we bury it, and it is no longer able to speak to us clearly.... Like a lamp that is behind a curtain, it begins to show us things more and more dimly, more and more darkly.... Thus we do not apprehend what our conscience tells us, and hence almost think that we do not have it. But there is no one who does not have it, and it is never lost."[36] Similarly, Abba Isaiah remarks that "when we do not obey our conscience, it withdraws and abandons us."[37]

Except in the rare instance of the saint, conscience is more or less buried in subconsciousness, and we are confronted with the problem of how conscience may be brought increasingly into our consciousness, so that its voice may be heard with more and more clarity; or, expressing the matter differently, of how conscience may be purified. The Byzantines offer pertinent counsel, stressing the need of complete obedience to conscience, constant inner attention and prayer.

In connection with obedience to conscience they emphasize the need of obeying conscience in all matters, not disobeying it in anything whatsoever, regardless how small and insignificant it might appear. "From small and trifling things," observes Abba Dorotheos, "we come to disregard big things. If, for instance, one begins to say: 'What does it matter if I say this? What does it matter if I eat this little thing? What does it matter if I look at that?' From this attitude of saying, 'What does it matter with regard to this?' and 'What does it matter with regard to that?' one develops a bad habit, and begins to disregard weightier things and to trample on his conscience. In this way one runs the danger of falling into complete unconsciousness (*anaisthēsia*) as far as conscience is concerned."[38]

Obedience to conscience is analyzed by Dorotheos, Symeon the New Theologian, and others into a threefold guarding (*phylakē*) of conscience: guarding it with reference to God, to man and to things. We guard conscience with reference to God when we follow all His commandments, neglecting none. We guard it in relation to man when we avoid wronging or scandalizing others in any way. Finally, we guard it in relation to things when we do not misuse them, but use all as is proper.

Essential for obeying one's conscience is inner attention. This practice makes it possible for one to apprehend the indications of conscience and avoid confounding them with thoughts and feelings alien to them. The ascetic-mystical Fathers frequently speak of inner attention and at times relate it to the awakening of conscience. Abba Isaiah says: "Let us not give any offence to our conscience, but observe ourselves with fear of God, until our conscience frees itself and a union between it and us takes place."[39] The union (*henōsis*) spoken of here is the entrance of conscience into our consciousness. A similar statement is made by Philotheos the Sinaite: "Attention," he says, "distinctly purifies conscience; and conscience having been purified, like a light that has been uncovered, shines brightly, driving away a great darkness."[40]

Prayer, especially mental prayer or prayer of the heart, is a most important means of awakening conscience as well as of regenerating the whole man. Mental prayer is prayer that is carried on by the mind or rational faculty when, having withdrawn from the realm of sensible things and concepts into the heart, it concentrates on the words of the prayer and their meaning, constantly repeating them. Mental prayer is also known as "pure prayer," because it presupposes a mind and heart free of all phantasies and alien thoughts. Mark the Ascetic says: "A good conscience is found through prayer."[41] Another Byzantine saint, John of Karpathos (probably 7th century), emphasizes the value of mental prayer, asserting that through it "our conscience is easily cleansed."[42] By means of such prayer we attract Divine grace within us; and it is this ultimately that effectively awakens conscience. According to Mark the Ascetic, "the *first* gift of Divine grace is the awakening of conscience."[43]

Besides the above mentioned practices for awakening conscience, there are many others of varying importance. Everything included in what the Greek Fathers call *ascesis,* "spiritual training," contributes to this great aim. Gregory Palamas, great champion of

Orthodox mysticism in the fourteenth century, points out that the soul is single yet with many powers; and that these powers are not isolated, but interconnected, so that if one of them is in a bad state all the others will be correspondingly affected.[44] It follows that, in order to be truly successful in his efforts to awaken his conscience, a person must simultaneously strive also to cleanse his other faculties, the whole inner man.

CHAPTER FOUR

THE *PHILOKALIA*

Two books are known by the title of *Philokalia,* a Greek word meaning "love of the beautiful." One of them is a compilation from the writings of Origen, made in the fourth century by St. Basil the Great and St. Gregory Nazianzen. The other is an anthology of writings by some thirty ascetic-mystical Fathers, ranging from the fourth to the fifteenth century, edited by two modern saints of the Eastern Orthodox Church: St. Macarios Notaras (1731-1805), Archbishop of Corinth, and St. Nicodemos the Aghiorite (1749-1809). The full title of the second *Philokalia,* the one we are concerned with here, is *Philokalia of the Sacred Wakeful Individuals: Compiled from Our Holy and God-bearing Fathers, by Which the Mind is Purified, Illumined, and Perfected through Practical and Contemplative Ethical Philosophy.*

Macarios prepared the first text of the *Philokalia,* and when he visited the Holy Mountain of Athos in 1777, he gave it to the monk Nicodemos to complete and edit. Nicodemos added, among other things, an introduction and brief biographies of the Fathers whose writings are included in this book. He had it ready for the printer after two years, during which he also edited other manuscripts that Macarios had submitted to him: one entitled *Evergetinos* and another, *Concerning Continual Communion.* When all three were ready, Macarios took them and left for Smyrna, where he hoped he would find donors to pay for the printing. He was successful, and the three books were published in Venice. The *Philokalia* appeared in 1782; the other two, in the following year. John Mavrogordatos, prince of Moldo-Wallachia, financed the printing of the *Philokalia.* His name appears on the title page of this monumental work of 1,207 folio pages.

The *Philokalia* was destined to exert a profound influence on the spiritual life, first of Greece, and soon of the entire Orthodox world. It was reprinted in Constantinople in 1861, and in Athens in 1893 and again in 1900; and the first part of a new five-volume edition was published in Athens in 1957.[1] The impact of the *Philokalia* on the Slavonic world was so strong that eleven years after its publication a Slavonic version came out in Moscow under the title of *Dobrotolubiye*. The translator was the Russian monk Paissy Velichkovsky, who had gone to Mount Athos in 1746, stayed there for seventeen years, and then settled in Moldavia. He and his disciples are credited with the spiritual revival that took place in Russia at the end of the eighteenth and the beginning of the nineteenth centuries. Between 1876 and 1890, a five-volume Russian version of the *Philokalia* was published. The translation was made by the Russian bishop Theophan the Recluse with the help of some monks of the Monastery of Optino and the Theological Academy of Moscow. The strong influence of the *Philokalia* upon the Russians is also manifest in *Candid Narratives of a Pilgrim to His Spiritual Father* (Kazan, 1884). This work, which appeared in English under the title of *The Way of A Pilgrim,* one of the finest and most popular manuals of Eastern Orthodox spirituality, was written in the second half of the nineteenth century by an unknown author inspired by the *Philokalia.*

In recent years the *Philokalia* has appeared in Roumanian, German, English, and French. The English version, in two volumes, was translated by E. Kadloubovsky and G. E. H. Palmer from the Russian. The first volume, entitled *Writings from the Philokalia on Prayer of the Heart,* was published in 1951, while the second volume, *Early Fathers from the Philokalia,* came out in 1954.

The Greek *Philokalia* comprises the work of about thirty writers, most of them saints of the Eastern Church, some well known, others less, some anonymous. The sequence in which they are presented is on the whole chronological. The Slavonic *Dobrotolubiye* is an abridged version of the *Philokalia,* containing fewer than half the authors. They are arranged according to type rather than in strictly historical sequence.

The Russian *Dobrotolubiye* is appreciably larger than the Greek *Philokalia.* Although it entirely omits four of the authors in the

Philokalia, some chapters by Palamas, and two of the anonymous texts, it adds nine other writers. The order in which they appear is different again from that of the Greek *Philokalia.*

The English version of the *Philokalia* in two volumes consists of selections from volumes I, II, III, and V of the Russian *Dobrotolubiye.*

In the study of the *Philokalia* that follows, I shall rely on the Athens edition of 1893. This includes all the texts contained in the first edition, arranged in the same order, plus some extra chapters by the Patriarch Callistos. It is divided into two folio volumes. My aim is to indicate and briefly interpret some of the main ideas contained in it.

To help man attain his own highest perfection is the ultimate goal of the *Philokalia.* The methods, both physical and spiritual, for attaining this end, are its principal matter. The path to be followed is spoken of as "the science (*epistēmē*) of sciences and the art (*technē*) of arts."

To understand this art or science one must have some acquaintance with the concept of human nature it presupposes. Man is seen as God's supreme creature: everything was created for him. "Man alone of all creatures," says St. John Damascene, "is in the image and likeness of God."[2] The terms "in the image" (*kat' eikona*) and "in the likeness" (*kath' homoiōsin*) are given a distinct meaning in the *Philokalia.* "Every man," says this saint, "is in the *image* of God, because of his possession of reason (*nous*) and of a soul which is incomprehensible, invisible, immortal, free, fit for rule, creative. . . . But very few men are in the *likeness* of God: only the virtuous and saints, who imitate God's goodness so far as is possible for man."[3] Similarly St. Diadochos of Photike (mid-fifth century) remarks: "All men are in the image of God, but only those are in His likeness, who through much love have made their freedom subservient to God."[4]

Man is a dual being, composed of body (*sōma*) and soul (*psychē*). The soul is an incorporeal, rational, immortal substance (*ousia*), superior to the body. "It does not occupy a place," says St. Gregory Palamas, "but neither is it everywhere. . . . It is throughout the body, not as being in a place, nor as being contained, but

as holding the body together, containing it, and giving life to it."[5]
The soul sustains all the members of the body, gives life to them,
and moves them. When it parts from the body, the body dies.[6]

The soul has diverse faculties or powers (*dynameis*), including
reason, will, conscience, and imagination. Reason, usually referred
to as *nous* or *logistikon,* has two distinct aspects, the contemplative
or intuitive, generally called *nous,* and the discursive, most often
denoted by the term *dianoia.* Palamas distinguishes between the
essence (*ousia*) of the rational faculty and its "energy" or operation
(*energeia*). The energy consists of thoughts, while the essence is
the power that produces these. Reason is the highest faculty in man.
It is the governor (*kybernētēs*) or master (*autokratōr*) of the whole
man, free in its activity. It is the faculty not only of knowledge,
but also of inner attention or observation and of contemplation.
It can observe itself as well as what is distinct from itself. Its power
of attention renders it the guardian of the whole man. Through
attention, *nous* observes evil and undesirable thoughts, images, and
feelings, and opposes them. The highest activity of the rational
faculty is pure prayer. In its truly natural state, reason can intui-
tively apprehend higher truth and behold the uncreated Divine
light. It is in its natural state when it is pure, free of bad or useless
thoughts and feelings. Such reason is very rare; it is possessed only
by saints. Hence, strictly speaking, they alone are truly rational.
"For one to be or become rational (*logikos*) in accordance with
nature, as man originally was," says St. Gregory the Sinaite, "is
impossible before the attainment of purity and incorruptibility. . . .
They alone are rational who through purity have become saints."[7]

The will (*thelēsis, boulēsis*) is an active power characterized
by the freedom of choice, the freedom to incline either towards the
good or towards evil. A free act of the will, whereby it surrenders
itself to the Divine will, is the beginning of the process of salvation
(*sōtēria*). St. Peter Damascene remarks: "Free choice is the beginning of salvation. This choice consists in man's giving up his own
volitions and thoughts, and doing the thoughts and volitions of
God."[8] "The ascent and deification of the will," says St. Theodore
of Edessa, "consists in its complete and continuous inclination and
movement towards the Supremely Beautiful."[9] The turning of the

will towards God comes as a free act of the human will, not as a result of divine constraint. In his fallen state, man needs Grace to *strengthen* the will's inclination and movement upwards; but the initial act of turning from the lower to the higher must come from man, his freedom being inviolable.

Conscience occupies a very important place in the *Philokalia.* This faculty is a true teacher that counsels excellently as to what is conducive to our salvation. It tells us what we ought to do, what our duties and obligations are. According to St. Mark the Ascetic, "Conscience is a natural book and he who reads it and follows it in practice gains the experience of divine perception."[10] Conscience resists acts that are contrary to nature, and censures the men who perform them. In man's ordinary state, conscience is more or less inoperative, having been separated from consciousness. It needs to be awakened and united with the rest of man's faculties. Conscience is awakened by Divine grace; but grace operates in proportion as we live in accordance with the Commandments. Also, except in the case of the saint, conscience is impure. Its purification is effected especially through inner wakefulness or attention combined with prayer.

The imagination (*phantasia*) is one of the lower psychical faculties of man; operating in a realm between reason and sense, it is also the possession of irrational animals. Imagination is divided into proper and improper. The first is accessory to meditation, as when one conjures up a picture of the Final Judgment in order to escape from base and evil thoughts. Improper imagination is that which is occupied with worldly, demonic, and unbecoming things. Imagination is one of the main obstacles to pure prayer, which requires an undistracted mind. It is also the chief instrument evil spirits use in leading man to wrong thinking, wrong feeling, and wrong doing. This is effected through suggestion (*prosbolē*). If suggestion is not consciously observed by means of inner attention and opposed by the mind, it results in an identification (*syndyasmos*) with it, then in consent (*synkatathesis*), and finally in the sinful act (*praxis tēs hamartias*). In striving to practice pure prayer of the heart, say the Fathers of the *Philokalia,* one should suppress the imagination entirely, not only improper, but proper imagination as well. That is, the mind must be kept free of all images, both good and bad.

What is said in the *Philokalia* about reason, the will, conscience, the imagination, and other powers shows that man in his ordinary, so-called normal state, is far from being what he ought to be. He is separated from higher truth and the Divine by various forms of impurity, and kept chained to lower levels of experience and being. Man is in need of what the Wakeful Fathers call the "beautiful" or "good" change (*alloiōsis*), which is growth in likeness to God leading to union with Him, to deification. This change is to be brought about by means of "work" (*ergasia*) or "training" (*askēsis*). Bodily "work" consists of such practices as fasting, continence, vigils, prostrations, and standing motionless at prayer. Spiritual "work" consists of concentration, meditation, inner attention, mental prayer and other interior practices. The expression "Practical and Contemplative Ethical Philosophy," which appears in the subtitle of the *Philokalia,* refers to such bodily and spiritual work.

In order to bring about the desired transformation, "work" must be performed with great diligence and energy, enough to cause painful sensations. Hence the bodily and spiritual practices are often referred to as "voluntary suffering" (*hekousioi ponoi*). The necessity of performing these activities so intensely as to produce painful sensations is very clearly indicated in the following passage by St. Gregory the Sinaite: "No work, whether bodily or spiritual, which lacks pain or effort, ever produces fruit. For 'the kingdom of heaven suffers violence,' says the Lord, 'and the violent take it by force.' By violence He means painful bodily feeling in all our efforts."[11]

The *Philokalia,* however, is chiefly concerned with spiritual practices, and it is with these and their results that we shall deal in the remainder of this study. Of the bodily practices, it will only be noted that the writers in the *Philokalia* regard them as important instruments for the spiritual practices, but of no value in themselves.

Concentration (*synagōgē*) as a mental practice is of fundamental importance, an essential component in the arts of meditation, inner attention, and mental prayer. The rational faculty has the tendency to wander about (*meteōrizesthai*) in "the world," to be distracted by sense-objects, images, and thoughts. Christ, we are reminded, urges us to avoid this wandering. "Our Lord," says St. Symeon the New Theologian, "tells us in the Holy Gospel: 'Avoid being distracted (*mē meteōrizesthai*)'; that is, do not scatter your mind hither and thither. And in another place He says: 'Blessed are the poor in spirit'; that is, fortunate are those who have not acquired in their heart any care about this world, but are destitute of every worldly thought."[12] Concentration is the withdrawing of the mind from the external world, turning it inward, gathering it into the heart. The effect of concentration is an intensification of the mind's contemplative power. With regard to this point, Callistos the Patriarch (fl. 1360) observes: "In proportion as the mind draws itself together, it becomes receptive of greater things. And when, drawing together all its movements, whether discursive, intuitive, or any other whatsoever, it restrains them, then it beholds that which is great beyond all else: God. And it beholds Him in proportion as the all-holy Grace of the Spirit grants, and as the nature of that which inhabits matter and is created can see Him Who is outside these."[13]

Withdrawing from worldly objects into the heart, the mind should meditate, exercise inner attention and pray. Meditation (*meletē*) is the focusing of the mind on God, death, judgment, hell, heaven, the lives of saints, the words of Christ, the apothegms of the Fathers, and the like. Regarding meditation on God, St. Peter Damascene says: "One ought to meditate on the name of God more often than one breathes, at every time and place, and whatever one is doing."[14] And St. Symeon the New Theologian advises: "Have the mind always turned to God, both in sleep and while awake, both when you are eating and when you are talking, both when you are doing manual work or are engaged in any other activity."[15] Such meditation causes one to rejoice within, forgetting worldly afflictions and becoming free from cares. Meditation on death is connected with meditation on the judgment, heaven and hell. "He who has acquired memory of death as a companion," remarks the same Father, "will seek with painful efforts to learn

what awaits him after his departure from this life."[16] This meditation results in non-attachment (*aprospatheia*) to present things,
indispensable for perfect knowledge of future things. Insofar as
it consists in remembering God, meditation is an essential element
of prayer. Otherwise it is a *preparation* of the mind for prayer.
"When the mind has become languid from [long continued]
prayer," says Theoleptos (fl. 1325), "renew its power by means of
reading and meditation, and make it readier for prayer."[17]

The highest form of spiritual work is mental prayer (*noera
proseuchē*), prayer of the heart (*kardiakē proseuchē*), or pure
prayer (*kathara proseuchē*). This form of prayer is called "mental
prayer" because it is carried on by the mind or spiritual faculty;
"prayer of the heart," because the mind engages in it while concentrated in the heart; and "pure prayer," because it presupposes
a mind and heart free of fantasies and thoughts. During this prayer,
one invokes Jesus Christ, saying, "Lord Jesus Christ, Son of God,
have mercy upon me." Hence it is also known as "the Jesus Prayer"
(*euchē Iēsou, epiklēsis Iēsou*). Mental prayer should be practiced
as far as possible incessantly, not only by monks, to whom the
Philokalia is especially addressed, but by all Christians, in accordance with the precept of the Apostle Paul in the First Epistle to
the Thessalonians to "pray without ceasing." Although it can be
practiced at any place and in any posture, it is most easily and
successfully practiced — particularly by beginners — when one is
seated in a dark, quiet place, with the head lowered so that the chin
touches the chest. The reason such a place and position are best is
that they aid concentration, an essential for successful prayer. The
control of breathing is also of assistance in the practice of mental
prayer: holding the breath helps one gather the mind together in
the heart and concentrate on the words of the prayer. At each
drawing of the breath one utters mentally the words: "Lord Jesus
Christ, Son of God, have mercy upon me;" and one holds the
breath a little. To be really fruitful, this prayer must be practiced
continuously and in the right manner over a long period. One
cannot practice it correctly unless he carefully follows the instruc-
tion in authoritative books and has the guidance of a wise and
experienced guide and teacher.

The first notable result of this prayer is pleasant warmth (*thermē*) of the heart, which purifies man of passions, effecting a state of passionlessness. This warmth is a manifestation of God, of Divine love. It "is the fire which our Lord Jesus Christ came to cast upon the earth of our hearts," remark Callistos and Ignatios Xanthopoulos.[18] The "passions" constitute a dividing wall (*mesoteichon*) between the heart and God, which darkens it and separates the mind from God. The overcoming and uprooting of the passions, the removal of the dividing wall or barrier, in a word passionlessness, opens the heart and mind to God. Through the opening of the heart (*kardiakon anoigma*) the Divine light enters us. First, then, comes warmth of the heart, then illumination (*phōtismos*) or effulgence (*ellampsis*). Illumination is "an ineffable energy, which is seen invisibly and known unknowably,"[19] according to Callistos and Ignatios. Palamas, who deals most extensively with illumination, says: "The Divine and deifying effulgence and grace is not the essence of God, but His uncreated energy (*aktistos energeia*)."[20] This light is also identified by him and other Fathers with the beauty (*kallos*) of God. The title of the *Philokalia,* which, as we have noted, means "love of the beautiful," is due in part to this identification. Our love (*philia, agapē, erōs*) should be directed above all to God, Whose most entrancing aspect is that of ineffable beauty. Callistos and Ignatios quote St. Basil the Great on this point: "What is more wonderful than the Divine beauty? What conception of God's magnificence is more glorious? What aspiration of the soul is so ardent and unbearable as that which is engendered by God in a soul which has been purified of every vice and which from a true disposition says: 'I am wounded by love?' "[21] The book is also termed "love of the beautiful" because it is directed to the virtues, which the writers in it view as beautiful qualities, that reflect the beauty of God.

Through prayer of the heart a union (*henōsis*) is achieved of man with himself and with God. Warmth of the heart, by consuming the passions, which are dividing forces, brings about the integration of the powers of the soul. Also, this warmth, being Divine love or grace appropriated in us, unites the soul with God. Similarly illumination, as a vision of, and union with, the Divine light, is a union with God, Who is light. Union with God, or *theōsis,* admits of degrees, depending on the capacity of receiving it, that is on purity of soul. Perfection with respect to such union is of two levels, the relative and the absolute. The latter is not attainable in this life, for while here we cannot contain divine perfection in its fullness.

These fruits of interior prayer are impossible without inner wakefulness (*nēpsis*) or attention (*prosochē*). Evagrios of Pontos (died 399) remarks: "Prayer which is not practiced in a wakeful, vigilant state is really futile."[22] To be effective, prayer must be pure; and it is pure when the imagination is suppressed, and the mind and heart are free of thoughts, images, and passions. As inner attention brings about these results, it is characterized by St. Nikephoros the Solitary (fl. 1340) as "the beginning of contemplation, or rather the foundation of contemplation."[23] Inner wakefulness is a higher level of consciousness (*aisthēsis*), transcending ordinary consciousness, which is really a state of inner sleep (*hypnos*), of unawareness (*anaisthēsia*). Our ordinary waking consciousness is a passive state of inner sleep, in that it is characterized by lack of a detached awareness of the contents or events of our mind, heart, and imagination, and the promptings of conscience. Inner wakefulness is an active state of mind, characterized by an objective awareness of these, that is, by self-observation, self-awareness. Because the writers in the *Philokalia* stress this fact and dwell upon the practice of inner wakefulness or *nēpsis,* they are called, as in the title of the *Philokalia,* "Wakeful Fathers," *Nēptikoi Pateres.*

Concerning the manner in which inner wakefulness or attention should be joined to prayer of the heart, Symeon the New Theologian says: "Attention must be so united to prayer as the body is to the soul. . . . Attention must go forward and observe the enemies like a scout, and it must first engage in combat with sin, and resist the bad thoughts that come to the soul. Prayer must follow attention, banishing and destroying at once all the evil thoughts which attention previously fought, because by itself attention cannot destroy them."[24] When all distracting inner factors have been done away with, then our whole attention should be turned to the words of the prayer. Thus practiced, this prayer leads to a level consciousness higher than that of *nēpsis*. *Nēpsis* is a consciousness of oneself, while the experience of warmth of the heart and the vision of the Divine light to which prayer of the heart leads is a consciousness of God.

CHAPTER FIVE

AESTHETIC EXAMINATION OF BYZANTINE ART

For centuries medieval Christian art — architecture, painting, poetry, music — was ignored or misinterpreted, was regarded as a lower, almost barbaric form of art. Although this attitude has changed in recent times, still medieval Christian art has not been properly understood and hence sufficiently appreciated. This is especially true of Byzantine art, the art that flourished in the Byzantine Empire from the fourth to the fifteenth century, and which down to the present day has been the art of the Greek Orthodox Church.

Panayiotis A. Michelis, professor of theory of architecture at the National Technical University at Athens and foremost modern Greek aesthetician, undertakes an aesthetic analysis and justification of Byzantine art in his book *An Aesthetic Approach to Byzantine Art*.[1] Byzantium has been condemned as "artistically inferior and sterile," says Michelis. But this charge, he holds, is very unjust. Byzantium was artistically very creative and its works of art are equal to those that have been produced by other great civilizations. Michelis undertakes to prove this by examining Byzantine architecture and painting with the technical equipment of modern aesthetics. He suggests that the same could be shown by examining the other arts of Byzantium, especially its religious music and poetry.

Let us see how Michelis proceeds to develop his argument. He begins by pointing out that in order to determine whether or not the art of a particular place or epoch is outstanding, we must judge it by the proper criteria. If our criteria are not appropriate, then our judgments will be amiss. This is what has occurred in the case of most modern aestheticians who have expressed their opinions on Byzantine art and, more generally, on the art of the Middle Ages. Byzantine art and medieval Christian art in general had for centuries been regarded "as inferior and not worthy of being called art in comparison with the art of Classical Antiquity, the art of the Italian Renaissance, and the subsequent art of the Neoclassical period." Moliere, for example, called the Gothic cathedrals "horrible monsters of ignorant centuries." Hegel characterized Byzantine painting as lifeless and of inferior craftsmanship, while Vischer stigmatized the figures depicted in Byzantine icons as "mummies." Why? Because, says Michelis, they judged them by the criteria of the humanistic mentality. They thought that all works of art must fit in the same mold. Whatever did not fit in it they rejected. For them a work that did not conform to the requirements of classical art was not a work of art.[2]

Michelis undertakes to vindicate Byzantine art on the basis of a well-defined system of aesthetic categories. He maintains that the misinterpretation of Byzantine art is due to the recognition of only one basic aesthetic category, that of beauty, of which the other aesthetic categories, such as grace and sublimity, are only "modes." It is not true that there exists only one aesthetic category: there exist six. These are the beautiful, the sublime, the tragic, the comic, the ugly, and the graceful. That is, "every artistic synthesis has a specific character: we call the work beautiful, sublime, tragic, comic, ugly, or graceful." This specific character is termed an "aesthetic category."

Of these aesthetic categories, the sublime and the beautiful are *basic, opposed,* and *equal in value.* The other four participate essentially in one or the other or both of these.

Now Byzantine art is dominated by the category of the sublime. And since this is basically different from the category of the beautiful, when a person criticizes Byzantine art because it lacks the beauty that characterizes the works of Classical Antiquity or of the Italian Renaissance, he commits a basic fallacy.

The study of the history of art, says Michelis, shows that there are three kinds of epochs, and that each of these is dominated by one definite aesthetic category. There are *anthropocentric* epochs, that is, epochs in which man dominates the scene. There are other epochs, which are *theocentric,* where there is a domination of the Divine. And there are epochs that are *transitional.* "Each transitional period . . . from theocentrism towards anthropocentrism *humanizes the gods.* And every transitional epoch from anthropocentrism towards theocentrism *deifies men,* and thus prepares psychologically for the turn to its antithesis." Now the anthropocentric epochs are dominated by the category of the beautiful; the theocentric, by the category of the sublime; and the transitional, by the category of grace. These epochs succeed one another. Epochs which are dominated by the categories of the tragic, the comic, or the ugly do not exist.

All this Michelis attempts to prove both inductively and deductively. He holds that Greek Antiquity was an anthropocentric period, and that its art expresses chiefly the beautiful. The same is true of the Renaissance. The Medieval period was theocentric, and its chief aesthetic category was the sublime. It was preceded and accompanied by a Rococo period, which was dominated by the category of grace. Underlying this argument is the thesis that there is an essential relation between the religious and philosophical outlook of an age and its art. Michelis maintains that art expresses in aesthetic symbols man's ideas and experiences regarding the great problems of God, Man, and the Cosmos; and its development follows fatefully the upward or downward course of these ideas and experiences.

Let us now see what sublimity is and how, as the dominant aesthetic category of Byzantium, it expresses the ideas and the experiences of the Byzantines regarding the great problems. What the "sublime" is can be understood better by comparing it with the "beautiful." The difference between the beautiful and the sublime can be explained in two ways: we can either indicate the respective intrinsic qualities of the beautiful and the sublime, or we can describe how the aesthetically sensitive person reacts towards them. If we examine works expressing these two categories, we shall see that in the beautiful there is a primacy of form, of measure, of the static, of quality, of the synthesis of antitheses, whereas in the sublime there is a primacy of the formless, of the unmeasured, of the dynamic, of quantity, of the resolution of antitheses. If, on the other hand, we turn our attention to our responses to these two categories, we shall observe the following. Towards

1.   Hagia Sophia. 532-7. South View. Constantinople.
(*Photo by Constantine Cavarnos.*)

the beautiful we feel serenity; towards the sublime, exaltation.
Towards the beautiful we feel delight; towards the sublime, wonder.
Again, the beautiful appeals more to our intellectual side; the sublime, more to our emotional side. Finally, the beautiful leads us
towards the outer world; the sublime, towards the inner world.

Byzantine art, says Michelis, as *Christian art par excellence,*[3]
is dominated by the category of the sublime. The Byzantines were
Christians, and their Christianity was deep. The religious lyricism
of the Byzantines overflowed their souls, because "both collectively
and individually they raised their souls towards heaven. They
believed in transcendent realities, in Divine persons, in the holy
history, in the miraculous, as though these were the only reality."
Their Christianity was directed inwards, was mystical. It was not a
religion of the external, material world, but a religion of the inner,
spiritual world. Important for them was not life here, but the life
beyond this. Earthly life was for them "but a trial journey."

Now Byzantine art employs various means in order to express
the religious faith of the Byzantines and their aspiration towards

2. Saints Theodore. XIth century. West View. Athens. (*Photo by Constantine Cavarnos.*)

the Divine. In architecture it succeeds in doing this through the proper use of space and light. The Byzantine architect was more concerned with the decoration of the interior of the church than with that of the exterior. Externally the Byzantine church is relatively plain, free of all superfluity, while inside it has an unsurpassed wealth of decoration. (See Figs. 1, 2.) As a Christian church, it "could not be, like the temple of the heathens, a dwelling of a god according to the prototype of the dwellings of men, that is, a mansion built out of marble, but had to become a miniature of the universe, because in it dwells the one and only God." The Byzantine architect succeeded in producing such an effect (a) by employing the principle of dematerialization — concealing the masses, polishing the surfaces or perforating them so that they looked like embroidery (e.g. the capitals, the lintels, etc.), and making many of the surfaces curved, causing by these means the materials to lose their heaviness and crassness (See Fig. 3); (b) by emphasizing the length and height of the building, unifying the inner space; and (c) by making proper use of sunlight. In the case of the basilica, there is a graded towering of the three or five roofs, and an intense illumination at the nave, producing a sense of religious exaltation. (See Figs. 4, 5.) In the case of the domed church, a similar effect is produced by the gradual rise of the vaults that support the dome and the piercing of the dome with windows. This upward movement "raises the gaze and the spirit of the spectator towards the light. Thus, in a likeness of the universe, the infinite but unified space is clearly exhibited as a bearer of the sublime idea of the omnipresent Divine Spirit." (See Fig. 6.)

In iconography, likewise, the Byzantines emphasized spirituality. By covering up with clothes the anatomically distorted body, by the stiffness of the representations, by the indifference to the ugliness of a person's characteristic features, the Byzantine painter accentuates "the inwardness of the representations and impresses the spectator with the idea that these beings have forgotten their body. . . . " The icon painter is not afraid to distort the natural proportions of the body, to exaggerate the size of some parts and diminish that of others, because in this way he expresses inner qualities. He is indifferent to the correct proportions of the body, to the *outer* form of man, because he wants chiefly to represent the *inner* man. All the expression of the soul is concentrated in the face. "The interest of the onlooker is withdrawn from the body and focused on the face and especially on the eyes. . . . " Here are expressed the virtues of meekness, humility, purity, spiritual love and wisdom, and so on. (See Figs. 7, 8.)

Byzantine art, says Michelis, does not express simply Christianity; it expresses the *Hellenic* conception of Christianity. This can be seen by a comparison of Byzantine with classical Greek art on the one hand and Gothic art on the other. Ancient Greek art is characterized by simplicity, clarity, idealism; Gothic art, by complexity, lack of clarity, uniqueness of form. Now Byzantine art does not lapse into complexity: it has *simplicity*. Nor does it lapse into vagueness: it has *clarity*. And it combines uniqueness of form with idealism: it has *measure* and *rhythm*. Both Byzantine and Gothic art express the sublime, but they do so differently: Byzantine art blends the sublime, which it took from the East, from Christianity, with the beautiful, which it inherited from Greece, whereas Gothic art expresses the sublime without the beautiful.

3. Capital. Church of Hagia Sophia, Constantinople. (*Photo by Pericles Papahatzidakis, Athens.*)

But is it possible for a work of art to express simultaneously the two fundamental and opposed aesthetic categories, the sublime and the beautiful, without being deprived of organic unity, without

4. Saint Demetrios. Vth century. Southwest side, as restored after fire of 1917. Thessaloniki. (*Photo by Pericles Papabatzidakis.*)

5. Saint Demetrios. Interior, as restored. Thessaloniki. (*Photo by Pericles Papapatzidakis.*)

6. Hagia Sophia, Constantinople. (*Drawing by Gaspard Fossati,* 1852.)

becoming falsified? Michelis anticipates this objection and provides an affirmative answer. A work of art, he says, *can* unite in itself elements or characteristics of different aesthetic categories, provided it is *dominated* by *one* aesthetic category. Byzantine art has the marks of the beautiful, but it is dominated by the category of the sublime. In this resides its originality.

This answer does not seem to me sufficient. I would add the following explanation. The "sublime" and the "beautiful" are

7.   St. Basil the Great and St. Gregory Nazianzen. Detail. Middle of XVIth century. Fresco in the eastern apse of the Church of Kaisariani, near Athens. (*Photo by Constantine Cavarnos.*)

not two fundamentally different aesthetic categories if considered formally, but only if considered materially, that is, with respect to the level of being they represent. By the "sublime" is meant inner or spiritual beauty, and by the "beautiful" is meant outer or physical beauty. Both are distinguished by the same formal characteristics: simplicity, measure, clarity, harmony, and the like. Spiritual beauty differs from physical beauty in that it belongs to a *higher level* of being than the latter. To use the language of Plato, spiritual beauty belongs to the level of *intelligible* things or *true being,* whereas physical beauty belongs to the level of *sensible* things or *phenomena.*

It is worth noting that Michelis himself sometimes employs the term "inner beauty" or similar expressions to refer to the sublime, and contrasts this beauty with that which is "outer." Referring, for instance, to the first Christians, he observes that "the spell of *outer* form stopped the moment when human nature was discovering another *beauty within* it." And elsewhere he remarks that in Byzantine iconography "facial ugliness is not avoided, but utilized whenever the supremacy of the *beauty of the soul* is thereby emphasized. . . ." In such cases "ugliness plays the role of repelling us momentarily, yet by this very fact compelling us to take note of the expression of *inner beauty.*"

The distinction between inner or spiritual beauty and outer or physical beauty is far from being new. It is encountered in many religious, philosophical, and other writings of Antiquity and the Medieval period. The view that spiritual beauty or the sublime is *superior* to physical beauty is closely connected with this distinction, and is implicit in the view that the soul is superior to the body and that God is superior to the physical world.

Now if we take seriously the distinction between spiritual and physical beauty, we must, I submit, go beyond Michelis in giving Byzantine art its proper place in the history of art. If it is true that spiritual beauty or the sublime is a value superior to physical beauty, and that — as Michelis argues and as I am convinced — Byzantine art has as its direct aim to express the sublime and succeeds in this aim to a superlative degree, then we are led to the conclusion that Byzantine art is not simply equal in value to the art of Classical Antiquity and of the Renaissance, but is superior.

Certain other considerations lead us to the same conclusion. Examining Byzantine art from the standpoint of aesthetics, Michelis dwells upon the aesthetic experience that Byzantine art elicits, not upon the effects it has on the moral and spiritual nature of man. Now Byzantine writers such as John Damascene, Theodore the Studite, Symeon of Thessaloniki and many others, looking at art from a psychological and religious rather than from an aesthetic standpoint, while recognizing the aesthetic experience evoked by

8. St. Barlaam. Detail. 1566. Fresco in the narthex of the Church of All Saints, Monastery of Barlaam, Meteora. (*Photo by Pericles Papahatzidakis.*)

Byzantine churches and icons, regarded this experience as something secondary. For them these sacred art objects have an additional value, far more important than aesthetic experience. This value resides in the effects these objects have upon the moral and spiritual nature of those who contemplate them. The church building and the icon are regarded not merely as objects that delight us, but rather as vivid reminders of a reality beyond themselves, of things transcendent, supernatural, and as potent aids for our inner purification and transformation. The important thing about a church for the Byzantines is the fact that its form and beauty are such that they remind us of Heaven, of God, and of the soul as a temple of God to be made pure and to be adorned with every virtue. Similarly, the important thing about icons is that they cause us to recall the sacred persons and events depicted, and the truths of Christian religion, thereby arousing our moral and spiritual zeal, and reinforcing our efforts to imitate the sacred persons and live in the light of religious truth.[4] Classical and Renaissance art lack this important property. Such art evokes delight, aesthetic experience, but does not lead us beyond nature to the plane of spiritual reality, and thus fails to effect a transformation of our inner being.

CHAPTER SIX

ICONOGRAPHY

Many books and articles have been written in recent years about Byzantine iconography. With very few exceptions, however, these writings dwell chiefly on the historical and aesthetic aspects of the subject. Among those who have written about Byzantine iconography mainly with a view to its inner essence is Fotis Kontoglou (1895-1965), the foremost icon painter of modern Greece and one of her most important literary and religious writers. Although he had said noteworthy things about Byzantine iconography before, it was in 1943 that he began to write about this sacred art in an extensive and authoritative manner, seeking to explain its distinctive features and to show its great value. In 1943 he wrote a series of articles entitled *Akēlidōta Archetypa*, "Spotless Archetypes," which appeared in *Nea Estia,* the leading literary journal of Greece. Subsequently he wrote countless articles interpreting and defending Byzantine art. These articles were published in newspapers, periodicals, and encyclopedias. His endeavors to make Byzantine iconography better understood and appreciated culminated in the publication, in 1960, of his monumental two-volume work entitled *Ekphrasis tēs Orthodoxou Eikonographias,* "Expression (or Explanation) of Orthodox Iconography."[1] This book is at once a guide for the icon painter, teaching the technique of painting icons according to the Byzantine tradition and explaining how each sacred personage or sacred event should be depicted, and also an attempt to enable the general reader to penetrate to the deeper, spiritual essence of icons done according to this great tradition.

Kontoglou does not discuss Byzantine art in the language, or in accordance with the method, of modern secular philosophers and aestheticians. He speaks as an iconographer and religious

thinker who experiences profoundly the Byzantine spirit — the
ascetic and mystical spirit of Greek Orthodoxy. "Byzantine art,"
he says, "is for me the art of arts. I believe in it as I believe in
religion. Only this art nourishes my soul, through its deep and
mysterious powers; it alone quenches the thirst that I feel in the
midst of the arid desert that surrounds us. In comparison with
Byzantine art, all the others appear to me trivial, 'troubling themselves about many things, when but one thing is needed.' "

He emphasizes the simplicity, clarity, restraint, power, originality and great spirituality of Byzantine art. This art, he observes,
is "an art with the most powerful character and with the greatest
spirituality and originality."

But there are many, Kontoglou is aware, who think very
differently. They look down upon Byzantine art because it lacks
naturalness. He does not deny that Byzantine paintings and mosaics
lack what is called "naturalness." But he observes that a painting
is not good because it is "natural," in the sense of observing carefully the anatomical structure of the body and the principles of
perspective, but for other reasons. A work may look "natural and
precisely for that reason not be good." Thus the hands and feet
in a Byzantine icon may appear unnatural, yet they are truer, more
expressive, more artistic than the hands that have been painted,
say, by a Raphael.

Byzantine iconography, then, is not to be condemned for not
being naturalistic, realistic, or for not reproducing faithfully the
external world. For its aim is something very different. Byzantine
iconography has a religious function. It seeks to express spiritual
things in order thereby to help man penetrate the mysteries of the
Christian religion; it seeks to help man rise to a higher level of
being, to lift his soul to the blessedness of God.

Employing traditional religious terminology, Kontoglou makes
a sharp distinction between two kinds of art, the "secular," or
"carnal," and the "spiritual." "Secular" art is either *naturalistic* or
imaginative; that is, it either imitates nature, representing the "external aspect of man and of other creatures," or it creates arbitrary
images according to human imagination. In either case, such art is
elaborate and ostentatious. Examples of it are found in the works of

9. The Holy Virgin Mary and the Child Christ. Panel icon. 1961.
By Fotis Kontoglou and his pupil Constantine Georgakopoulos.
(*Courtesy Holy Transfiguration Monastery, Boston.*)

Raphael, Guido Reni, Carlo Dolci, Ingres, Renoir, and Picasso.

"Spiritual" art, on the other hand, does not imitate either nature, the material world, or the arbitrary creatures of man's imagination, but things belonging to the realm of the spirit, using sacred and symbolic forms and mystical colors. It is not elaborate and pretentious, but simple and humble. It does not serve human passions, but God. It is not individual, but universal, being guided not by personal, subjective preferences, or by the secular taste of the age, but by Tradition and Divine grace. An example of such an art is the Byzantine.

As I have already remarked, Kontoglou emphasizes the simplicity, the clarity, the restraint, and the power of Byzantine art. Take, he says, the Holy Virgin painted on Byzantine icons and compare her with the theatrical idol that has been painted in the West and called by the same name. The first is modest, solemn, venerable; the second is a "doll with rings and earrings and a whole lot of unholy and foolish things. . . . " Again, take the Nativity. "The Greek Orthodox iconographers have painted the Nativity of Christ with the mysticism that one feels who believes simply and truly, as a 'child,' according to the word of Christ." It has the same simplicity as the language in which the Gospels describe the event. It has forms and colors that are mystical, simple, unpretentious; it is expressive without being ostentatious, profound without being intricate. Take, on the other hand, the representation of the same event by many painters of the Western Church. The Nativity here has been painted elaborately, "like a theatrical setting, similar to those that one sees at the movies." "The paintings of Western iconography," observes Kontoglou, "represent a world foreign to the Gospels, especially the works that have been made by the painters of the Italian Renaissance. . . . " These latter, in particular, are devoid of religious contrition, devoid of all mystery, having been painted for the sake of displaying the artist's ability to paint things that appear natural, and for evoking aesthetic experience

Secular art is concerned with external beauty, whereas spiritual art is concerned with inner beauty. Kontoglou emphatically places inner, spiritual beauty above external beauty, and spiritual art above secular art. External, physical beauty, he remarks, is shallow and perishable, while spiritual beauty is deep and imperishable. Physical beauty arouses the outer senses; spiritual beauty, the inner senses — it makes us feel reverence, humility, contrition, the "gladdening sorrow" of which St. John Climacos speaks.

With regard to the creation of works of spiritual art, Kontoglou holds that there is presupposed a certain inward state. Such works, he believes, cannot be created "by any carnal man, even though he be the greatest master." They can be produced only by an artist, even though he be unlettered, who fasts, prays, and lives "in a state of contrition and humility." For only then is the soul "imbued with Grace, soars upward with spiritual wings, and becomes capable of representing the deep realm of mysteries."

Similarly, says Kontoglou, the beauty expressed by such works is not perceived by carnal, sophisticated, impious men any more than is the truth and beauty of "the Gospels and of everything that emits a spiritual fragrance." Such persons understand only the language of the senses; spiritual art, however, "does not address itself to the senses, but to the spirit." In order to apprehend spiritual beauty, one must have a special sensibility. This sensibility may be found not only in those who are cultured, but also in those who are not. Simple folk, observes Kontoglou, understand and appreciate Byzantine art, whereas the pseudo-cultured, who have lost their healthy simplicity and piety, do not; they despise it or at most regard it condescendingly as merely "fine archeology." Such persons, he says, "want to hear theatrical music in the churches and to behold ostentatious, rosy-cheeked icons. They do not like Byzantine architecture, music, and iconography, which sprang from the deep piety of the Orthodox, but want the Church to become a theater, and worship to become a stage performance.

I am reminded here of Leo Tolstoi. "A good and lofty work of art," says the Russian writer, "may be incomprehensible, but not to simple unperverted, peasant laborers (what is highest is understood by them)— it may be and often is unintelligible to erudite, perverted people destitute of religion. . . . "[2] But Kontoglou does *not* mean, as Tolstoi does, that all those who have not been perverted are *equally* capable of understanding and feeling spiritual art. Tolstoi remarks that art "acts on people independently of their state of development."[3] Kontoglou, on the other hand, holds that a person who has not only simplicity, that is, an integrated, un-perverted nature, but also a higher spirituality can appreciate the work better. In order fully to understand the work of an artist, he says, you must stand on the same level of purity, of development as he.

Kontoglou stresses, as I have noted, the power of Byzantine art. In the countries of Europe, he observes, paintings that are famous for their artistic merits are to be found in churches. Yet they do not have the power of touching us so profoundly as the works of some unlearned and unknown Byzantine painters. This quality is to be found not only in the paintings, he maintains, but also in the mosaics, churches, hymns, music and other works of art of the Byzantine or Greek Orthodox Tradition. For they all express, by different means, one and the same inner essence.

CHAPTER SEVEN

MANUEL PANSELINOS

At Karyes, the capital of the Holy Mountain of Athos, is the most important church of this unique Pan-Orthodox democracy of monks, belonging to all the Athonite monasteries: the Church of the Protaton. This church dates from 965, and is a basilica, the only main church of that type on the Holy Mountain.

The exterior of this edifice, which has recently been extensively repaired, is very simple, yet majestic. The ground plan is oblong. The side walls are perforated with tall round-arched windows, while those of the clerestory are pierced by similar small ones. The building leans over to the north side, and recently buttresses have been constructed on that side to carry the outward thrust. The interior has the form of a cross, which has been achieved by dividing the church from the bema to the narthex into three oblong sections: a broad one at the middle and a narrow one on each side, and cutting the side sections at the ends by means of walls, thus forming rectangular divisions at each end. The eastern arm of the cross is separated from the rest by the iconostasis.[1]

When one enters the Church of the Protaton, one is impressed by its length and height and by the superb frescoes that adorn its walls. All the walls, except those of the narthex, which appears to have been constructed or reconstructed at a later date, are decorated with frescoes that were painted at the beginning of the 14th century by one of the greatest masters of Byzantine iconography: Manuel Panselinos of Thessaloniki (Salonika). No description, even the most detailed and most eloquent, can give one an adequate idea of the beauty and power of these icons. These representations of sacred persons and incidents are not naturalistic, as some have asserted; nor are they products of man's arbitrary imagination. They are the forms of new, transfigured men, imprinted upon matter

10. St. Procopios. Detail. XIVth century. Fresco by Panselinos, Church of the Protaton. (*Photo by Fotis Zachariou, Athens.*)

11. St. Theodore Tyro. Detail. Fresco by Panselinos, Church of the Protaton. (*Photo by Fotis Zachariou.*)

by an artist who succeeded in rising above the realm of nature and the realm of imagination to that of the spirit.

What impresses the person who gazes at the figures depicted on the walls is the quality best described by the term spiritual grandeur. Their postures, gestures, and above all their faces express this quality in a striking manner: they express great seriousness of character, freedom from all pretense and servility, and great spiritual depth. Surrounded by these figures, one feels that he is in the presence not merely of paintings, but of beings far more real than persons that he meets in everyday life. These sacred figures bear the clear impress of complete self-mastery, inner purity, and freedom from everything petty, from all impatience and weakness. Everything about them bespeaks great calm and tremendous inner power. The contemplation of these icons introduces one into a new dimension of being. It makes one experience these sublime qualities, arouses one's admiration for them, and awakens and strengthens the desire to acquire them.

The traditional means of attracting the attention of the beholder to the face, where these qualities are especially expressed, have been employed with exceptional skill by Panselinos. Thus, the halo (*stephanos*) that surrounds the head has been made very large and has been set in bold relief by painting around it a red and then a white band, and setting the whole in a dark blue background.

Beauty, not loudness, characterizes the colors. Sometimes they show a striking disregard for nature. For example, a greenish hue has been used a great deal on the faces and other exposed parts of the body, especially at the edges. There is a large variety of colors, many of which are light. Blue has been employed frequently and extensively. Thus, the garments of many figures are blue, and the background is always dark blue. White also has been used very much, sometimes all by itself; sometimes in conjunction with black or brown: for instance, in the case of the garments of the Great Hierarchs (St. John Chrysotom, St. Gregory the Theologian, etc.), black and white, and brown and white have been employed to form a contrasted pattern of crosses; and frequently, in combination with other colors to form light hues, such as light green, light red,

12. St. Theoktistos. Detail. Fresco by Panselinos, Church of the Protaton. (*Photo by Pericles Papahatzidakis.*)

and light brown. In the representation of certain saints, such as St. Paul and the Athonite hermits, a simple combination of colors has been employed, whereas a greater variety of colors and much ornamentation has been used in the representation of the Hebrew and Christian king-saints.

The bodily form of the older figures differs markedly from that of the younger ones: the face and body of Christ and other younger figures are full, whereas the faces of the older saints, especially of the hermits of Athos, are thin, the cheeks sunken, and the bodies slender or even emaciated. But all the figures are large, so that even those on the uppermost of the four strips of frescoes that cover the walls of the church can be seen very distinctly by anyone with normal vision. These paintings were clearly meant to be not merely ornamental, but *liturgical*, that is, to be seen in all their details and to evoke religious experience.

Very little is known about the artist who executed these superb icons. In his remarkable book, *Explanation of the Art of Painting*, which was written about 1730, the icon painter Dionysios of Fourna says of Panselinos that "he shone with the full brilliance of the sun and surpassed all the painters, ancient and modern, as is shown most clearly by the icons which have been painted by him on walls and panels. This will be excellently realized by anyone who studies them and views them well, and has some knowledge of the art of painting."[2] Of Panselinos' panel icons, which Dionysios mentions, none survives. His frescoes in the church of the Protaton are his only extant works.

Chapter Eight

EL GRECO AND BYZANTINE PAINTING

A significant work on the celebrated Cretan painter Domenikos Theotokopoulos (1541-1614), commonly known as El Greco, was published in 1961, entitled *El Greco Revisited*.[1] The author of this work is Pal Kelemen, an American of Hungarian origin, well known for his studies on art, especially medieval art and Baroque and Rococo in Latin America. Kelemen bases himself in this book not only on various writings pertaining to El Greco, but also on his direct acquaintance with the Cretan's paintings as well as with the Byzantine monuments. His extensive study of Byzantine iconography enabled Mr. Kelemen to discern many elements of Orthodox, Byzantine art in the works of Theotokopoulos and to appreciate the great value of that art.

It is significant that from the very first page of his work the author stresses the importance of Byzantine art, both in itself and in relation to the art of the East and West. "Byzantine art," he remarks, "long misrepresented, if not ignored, in Roman Catholic and Protestant countries as an example of degenerate Christianity, shines each year more radiant through the reexamination made possible partly by a more enlightened attitude and partly by better facilities for travel and photography."[2] And a little later he says: "From Byzantine art not only a religious expression but also a spiritual experience can be drawn. But the enrichment comes all too belatedly for the Western world to benefit from it fully, because of the deluge of different religions and philosophies of the peoples of Asia and Africa...."[3] Kelemen goes on to assert that in earlier centuries "Byzantine art radiated throughout East and West,"[4] and that Byzantium "enriched the Western world for more than a thousand years with its spiritual, intellectual, and artistic achievements."[5] Byzantium had no "Dark Ages."[6] The picture of the Byzantine world which the English historian Gibbon gave in his book *The Decline and Fall of the Roman Empire* "was essentially a false one."[7]

The knowledge and appreciation of Byzantine art which Kelemen gained through study and trips to the Holy Mountain of Athos and other parts of Greece, as well as to Constantinople and elsewhere, made it impossible for him to ignore the question of the influence of Byzantine art on Theotokopoulos, who began to fascinate him several decades ago. His long study of El Greco and of Byzantine art led him to the conclusion that the Greek painter had mastered the art of the Byzantine tradition. This conclusion constitutes the chief thesis of his book *El Greco Revisited.*

In a note which was added to this book[8] some months after its release, Kelemen brings to the attention of the reader the fact that this thesis was fully justified by the congress which was held in the Cretan city of Heraklion (Candia) in September, 1961, shortly after the publication of his book. Most of those who have written about Theotokopoulos during the last hundred years have expressed the opinion that the famous painter was nineteen years old when he arrived in Venice, an untutored lad. Kelemen observes that nineteen was a man's age in those days, and that according to the announcement made at the congress in Heraklion, Theotokopoulos was still in his native land at the age of twenty-five, already a skilled artist. The announcement was made by C. D. Mertzios, archivist and historian and long-time vice-consul in Venice. Mertzios found a document from Heraklion dating from 1566, containing the signature of Theotokopoulos and next to it the word "painter."

The most important part of the book is the last chapter, where the author shows in detail the similarities which exist between the works of Theotokopoulos and the icons of the Byzantine style, as well as the differences that separate the works of El Greco from those of Western painters. The influence of Byzantine art is seen especially in the frequent use of Orthodox prototypes, both in the representation of isolated figures and in compositions; in the use of perspective in the Byzantine manner, which gives these works the impression of two-dimensionality instead of the three-dimensionality of Western Renaissance painting; and in the repetition of the same theme, as was customary with the Byzantine iconographers: "El Greco had nothing of the vanity of the Western painter when it came to repetitions."[9] One should add that the influence of Byzantine art is also conspicuous in El Greco's tendency to elongate the body, the fingers, etc. Such elongation is characteristic of Byzantine icons, particularly those belonging to the Cretan School.

As regards the use of Byzantine prototypes, Kelemen observes, for instance, that the depiction of Christ in Benediction is strongly reminiscent of the Byzantine Pantocrator, the all-seeing and all-knowing Judge. Not only the attitude of the body, but also His gestures, hair, and other details evince the Orthodox tradition, known as Byzantine. This Christ is the most Byzantine work of El Greco. (Cf. Figs. 13 and 14.) And St. John the Baptist as depicted by El Greco brings to mind the Baptist of Byzantine icons. He is tall and gaunt, his hair is curly and uncombed, his gaze sad, and his fingers long and thin. (Cf Figs. 15 and 16.) In the Apostle Paul, too, Kelemen sees the form of the Byzantine tradition. He calls attention to the Byzantine elements of various other works of Theotokopoulos, and refers the reader to the pertinent illustrations, where he may ascertain this by comparing the works of the Cretan painter on the one hand with icons of the Byzantine style, and on the other hand with panels by Western painters.

The following observations of Kelemen also help us understand the relation of El Greco to Byzantium: (a) That in the catalog of the books El Greco had in his library there are included 27 Greek works, of which 8 are religious, and all belong to the Orthodox world.[10] These books are the Old Testament, the New Testament, the homilies of Basil, the orations of John Chrysostom, *Concerning the Celestial Hierarchy* by Dionysios the Areopagite, Justin Martyr, the *Apostolic Constitutions,* and a work which is mentioned as St. Dionysios. (b) That "the library does not show one book by a Western Father, such as Augustine, Jerome, Gregory,[11] Ambrose...."[12] From these data we can draw the inference that during his stay in Spain El Greco was nourished spiritually by the Orthodox East, an inseparable manifestation of which is Byzantine iconography. "The old saying, 'Show me your books and I will show you who you are,' applies to El Greco."[13]

13. Christ. Panel icon. 1958. By Fotis Kontoglou. (*Photo by Z. Zapheiriou, Athens.*)

14. Christ in Benediction. By El Greco. Toledo, Spain. (*Courtesy Pál Kelemen.*)

15. St. John the Baptist. Panel icon. XVIth century.
Church of the Protaton, Mount Athos. (*Photo by Pericles Papahatzidakis.*)

16.   St. John the Baptist.   By El Greco.   (*Courtesy M. H.
de Young Memorial Museum, San Francisco.*)

17. The Baptism of Christ. Miniature. Xth century.
Manuscript 10, Monastery of Iviron, Mount Athos. (*Photo
by Pericles Papahatzidakis.*)

18.   The Baptism of Christ. By El Greco. Madrid.
(*Courtesy Pál Kelemen.*)

The influence of Byzantium is seen by Kelemen, not so much
in the total impression made by Theotokopoulos' paintings, as in
characteristic details which are reminiscent of the Byzantine heritage
of the Cretan painter, and which become more marked during his
residence in Toledo. This opinion is entirely justified. In the works
of El Greco there is present, besides the influence of Byzantium,
that of Western painting, as well as his personal impress. These
different elements give to El Greco's art a unique character. His
art is neither Byzantine nor Western, but a peculiar mixture of
Byzantine and Western art.

Kelemen recognizes the Western influence in the works of
Theotokopoulos, but does not undertake to enumerate and comment
on the Western elements that are discernible in them. By comparing, however, the paintings of El Greco with Byzantine icons
and with the works of the Italian Renaissance, we can notice that
there are many points where the Greek painter leaves the Byzantine
tradition and approaches Western art. Personally, I have noted the
following:

In the first place, the paintings of El Greco do not possess
the simplicity of Byzantine icons. One can see this if one compares
a composition of El Greco, such as the Baptism of Christ, with a
Byzantine composition depicting the same theme. The Baptism as
it is represented by El Greco is full of superfluous things, whereas
the representation of this event in a Byzantine icon is limited to
what is essential. Undue complexity and elaborateness is a characteristic of Western art, whereas simplicity and limitation to what
is essential is a distinguishing mark of Byzantine art. (Cf. Figs.
17 and 18.)

Secondly, the panels of El Greco that have religious themes
lack the hieraticalness and mystical calm of Byzantine icons, being
characterized by a certain theatricalness, sentimentality, and agitation.

Thirdly, Theotokopoulos often does not cover up the body
with clothes, whereas in Byzantine icons the body is rarely depicted
uncovered. For instance, Theotokopoulos' St. John the Baptist is
represented almost stark naked, both in the Baptism of Christ and
in a panel where he is depicted alone. And in the Baptism, the

Annunciation, and other works of El Greco we observe naked angels, as we see in the works of the Renaissance Italians, but not in Byzantine icons.

Fourthly, the representation of many figures of El Greco is not at all reminiscent of corresponding figures in Byzantine icons. For example, his Madonna in the Annunciation and elsewhere is not at all like the Byzantine Theotokos. She has neither her physiognomy nor her hieraticalness. She is a sentimental woman with an astonishingly small head, a type that seems to have pleased the Spaniards.

Fifthly, El Greco abandons the Byzantine style in depicting the folds of the garments and follows rather the Western.

Further, he does away with the *stephanos* or halo — the gold or yellow ochre disk that surrounds the heads of sacred persons in Byzantine icons. Here again he follows the Western Renaissance painters.

Finally, like the artists of the Renaissance who occupied themselves with religious themes, El Greco does not have the feeling that he is working under the inspiration and guidance of God, as the Byzantine iconographers had. The latter for this reason never signed their works, but either left them anonymous, or when they recorded their name always placed before it the term "Hand of" or "Through the hand of." Theotokopoulos does not have the feeling of a Divine factor in the execution of his works, but views them as purely personal creations. His name is seldom preceded by the words "Hand of." Almost always he puts his signature: "Domenikos Theotokopoulos," and usually adds the word "made."

There are, then, in my opinion, serious differences separating the art of Theotokopoulos from Byzantine iconography. Even though he painted many religious themes, he cannot be characterized as an icon painter. And his religious paintings cannot be regarded by the Eastern Orthodox as liturgical objects, as means of worship. They are in essence secular paintings with religious themes.

Judging the works of El Greco from the standpoint of spiritual expression, I submit that they should be placed lower than the works of Byzantine art, but higher than those of Western painters of the post-medieval period. The higher spiritual expression of the works of the Cretan painter is due to their Byzantine elements. And these, in turn, as Kelemen convincingly shows, are due to his apprenticeship to the Byzantine school when he was in his native land, and also to the fact that his long residence in the West never resulted in a severing of the ties which linked him with the spirituality of the Orthodox East.

Chapter Nine

SACRED MUSIC

Byzantine sacred music, which is the traditional, official music of the Greek Orthodox Church, is characterized, as far as its inner essence is concerned, by simplicity or freedom from undue complexity, by purity or freedom from everything sensual, ostentatious, insincere, and by unsurpassed power and spirituality. As regards its outer form or technical aspect, it is characterized by the fact that it is entirely vocal, not making use of any instruments, and monophonic, that is, employing melodies in one vocal part only.

That these qualities characterize Byzantine sacred music, and precisely how, will become evident in what follows, especially as I discuss its purpose and the manner of executing it.

The aim of this music is not to display the fine voices of the chanters, or to entertain the congregation, or to evoke aesthetic experience. Indeed, the chanters who sing it must have good voices, and the chanting must be well executed and pleasant to hear. However, the good voices and the good execution are not things it seeks for their own sake; and the pleasure it evokes is not an end it deliberately seeks, but something incidental, and, further, is not mere aesthetic pleasure but something much richer and higher. The aim of Byzantine sacred music is spiritual. This music is, in the first place, a means of worship and veneration; and in the second place, a means of self-perfection, of eliciting and cultivating man's higher thoughts and feelings and of opposing and eliminating his lower, undesirable ones.

The use of this music as a means of worship consists in employing it to glorify God, and to express feelings of supplication, hope, gratitude, and love to Him. Its use as a means of veneration consists in employing it to honor the Holy Virgin and the rest of the Saints. Its use as a means of cultivating higher thoughts and feelings and opposing the lower ones is inseparable from these. There is not one kind of music employed as a means of worshipping God and honoring the saints, and another kind employed for transforming our inner life, but the same music, while having as its direct aim the former, incidentally leads also to the fufillment of the latter. For while glorifying God and honoring the saints by means of psalms and hymns, or while listening to others chant while we do so in our hearts, feelings such as sadness, hatred, anger, and torpor subside, and feelings such as contrition, love, peace, and spiritual joy and aspiration are aroused.

From the very beginning, Christianity recognized the value of hymn- and psalm-singing as a means of *worship.* Christ and His disciples, as the Gospels testify, used it for this purpose. Matthew and Mark write that after the Mystical ("Last") Supper Christ and His disciples "sang a hymn" and went out to the Mount of Olives.[1] Luke, describing the same event in more detail, says: "As He was now drawing near, at the descent of the Mount of Olives, the whole multitude of the disciples began to rejoice and praise God with a loud voice for all the mighty works that they had seen, saying, 'Blessed be the King Who comes in the name of the Lord. Peace in heaven and glory in the highest!' "[2] And the Apostle Paul, writing to the Ephesians, tells them: "Sing and psalmodize to the Lord with your heart, always and for everything giving thanks in the name of our Lord Jesus Christ to God the Father."[3] Again, writing to the Colossians, Paul tells them to thank God by singing "psalms and hymns and spiritual songs."[4] And in his letter to the Hebrews he quotes the psalm of David: "I will proclaim Thy name to my brethren, in the midst of the church I will sing a hymn to Thee."[5] Finally, in the *Acts of the Apostles,* Paul and one of his chief fellow workers, Silas, are said to have employed chanting as a means of worship: "About midnight, Paul and Silas were praying and singing hymns to God, and the prisoners were listening to them. . . ."[6]

The recognition of sacred singing as a means of *spiritual development* also is to be found in the New Testament. Thus, Paul advises the Ephesians: "Do not get drunk with wine, for that is dissipation; but be filled with the Spirit, by singing among yourselves psalms and hymns and spiritual songs."[7] Here it is clearly implied that the practice of singing, or listening to, psalms, hymns and spiritual songs uplifts us spiritually and makes us recipients of the Holy Spirit. And in his letter to the Colossians he says: "Let the word of Christ dwell in you richly, as you teach and admonish each other in all wisdom by singing psalms, hymns, and spiritual songs."[8] That is, sacred singing is a means of educating and being educated in Christ's Divine wisdom.

The teaching of the Eastern Fathers on this subject, which is scattered in their numerous writings, is an elaboration of the ideas contained in the New Testament. Many of the great Fathers speak vividly of the employment of psalms, hymns, and spiritual songs as means of worship. In one of his letters,[9] St. Basil says: "What then is more blessed than to . . . hasten to prayer at daybreak, and to worship the Creator with hymns and songs?" St. John Damascene, in the fifth ode of the Easter Day Canon, says: "Let us arise at deep dawn, and instead of fragrant oil let us offer a hymn to our Lord." And St. Symeon the New Theologian says that every prayer and psalmody is a conversation (*synomilia*) with God in which we either entreat Him to give us those things which it is proper for God to give to men, or we thank Him for His gifts, or we glorify Him for all the creatures which He has made, or we narrate His wonderful deeds, which He performed at various times for the salvation of men and the punishment of the unrighteous, or we narrate the great mystery of the incarnation of the Son and Logos of God, and the like.[10] It should be noted that the term "psalmody" (*psalmōdia*), as used by Greek writers, does not mean psalm-singing only, but also ode- and hymn-singing.

Regarding the honoring of the saints by means of psalmody, John Damascene says that "We ought to honor the saints as friends of Christ, as sons and heirs of God, as John the Theologian and Gospel-writer says: 'As many as received Him, to them gave He power to become sons of God.'[11] 'Wherefore they are no more servants, but sons; and if sons, also heirs of God through Christ.' "[12] Now one of the ways this honor is to be rendered is by means of "psalms, hymns, and spiritual songs."[13] Again, the *apoyltikion* sung in honor of the three great teachers of the Church, St. Basil the

Great, St. Gregory the Theologian, and St. John Chrysostom, on the 30th of January, says in part: "Let us all who love their teachings, having assembled together, honor them with hymns, for they are ever making intercession to the Holy Trinity for us."

The Eastern Fathers have said many illuminating things about the great value which psalmody has as a means of inner purification and growth, of opposing and eliminating negative, useless, undesirable thoughts (*logismoi*), as well as negative, undesirable feelings, which they call passions, and of eliciting and nourishing the positive, higher, desirable thoughts and feelings. I shall give some examples. St. Athanasios the Great remarks that through psalmodizing, "the turbulence and roughness and disorder in the soul are smoothed away and sadness is overcome."[14] And a little later he observes that those who psalmodize properly "psalmodize not only with their tongue, but also with their mind, and benefit greatly not only themselves but also those who desire to listen to them. Thus the blessed David, chanting in this way to Saul, himself pleased God, and banished the turbulent and mad passion of Saul, and rendered his soul calm."[15] Similarly, in one of his letters,[16] St. Basil says: "The discipline of piety nourishes the soul with divine thoughts. What then is more blessed than to imitate on earth the sacred chorals of angels' choirs; to hasten to prayer at daybreak, and to worship the Creator with hymns and spiritual songs; and then, when the sun shines brightly and we turn to our tasks, praying being our companion at all places, to season our work with hymns as food with salt? For the state of the soul in which there is joy and no sorrow is a blessing bestowed by the consolation of hymns." And in another letter [17] he asserts that through psalmodizing one secures attention and keeps the mind from wandering. John Chrysostom, commenting on the 41st Psalm, says: "Nothing, nothing uplifts the soul so much, and gives it wings, and liberates it from the earth, and releases it from the fetters of the body, and makes it aspire after wisdom and deride all the cares of this life, as the melody of unison and rhythm-possessing sacred songs."[18] And commenting on the passage in Paul's Epistle to the Ephesians which I cited earlier, he says: "Those who psalmodize are filled with the Holy Spirit, just as those who sing satanic songs are filled with an unclean spirit."[19] Evagrios of Pontos observes that "Psalmody, long-suffering, and compassion stop the agitation of anger."[20] St. John Cassian (360-435) stresses the value that psalmody has, in conjunction with other means, of bringing about a purification of the mind. "The correction of our mind," he says, "is within our power and requires efforts on our part. For when we meditate on the Law of God continually and with understanding, sing psalms and sacred songs, and in addition practice fasting and vigils, . . . evil thoughts become fewer and do not find place in our mind."[21] St. Nilos the Ascetic teaches that "Psalmody puts the passions to sleep and stills the intemperance of the body."[22] St. John Climacos remarks that "Sometimes suitable psalmody extinguishes anger in a most successful manner."[23] And elsewhere he asserts that "according to the Fathers, psalmody is a weapon against evil thoughts."[24] Elsewhere again, speaking dramatically of spiritual torpor (*akēdia*), he has the demon of this vice confess: "My adversaries, by whom I am now held bound, are psalmody and manual work."[25] And in another place, speaking more generally, John says: "A noble horse, when it begins to run, warms up, and the more it runs the more it is wont to run. Now by running I mean hymnody, and by the noble horse I mean the mind (*nous*), which, sensing the [spiritual] warfare from afar and being prepared [by means of hymnody], remains always invincible."[26]

In order to succeed in fulfilling these important purposes, Byzantine church music must be executed in a certain manner. It must, in the first place, be chanted in a state of *attention* or *inner wakefulness,* with *fear of God, devoutness, contrition, humility.* Thus, the Synod in Trullo (691-692) ruled, in the 75th canon, that "those whose office it is to chant in the churches . . . offer the psalmody to God, Who is the observer of secrets, with great attention and contrition." And Chrysostom, commenting on the verse of the Apostle Paul: "With psalms, with hymns, with spiritual songs, with grace singing in your hearts to God," says that we are told here not to psalmodize simply with the mouth, but in a state of spiritual wakefulness: "For this constitutes singing to God — the other is merely singing to the air."[27] And Symeon the New Theologian says: "One must psalmodize, that is, pray with the

mouth, with fear and piety and attention."[28] Later on, he remarks:
"If they ask you to act as the canonarch of the choir, do not act
carelessly and lazily, but thoughtfully and with great attention, as
though you were spreading with your voice and hand the divine
words to your brethren, in front of the King of all, Christ."[29] And
in another place he observes that he who has become humble, as a
real Christian should be, "will sing a new hymn to the Lord, that
is, will offer thanks to God with a pure and contrite heart — for a
pure heart is one which is contrite and humble. Every other form of
psalmody besides this is vain and futile. For one who does not
psalmodize in this manner cannot converse with God through
prayer, even though he exert himself to this end a great deal. He
will psalmodize and say prayers with the tongue, but with his mind
he will be thinking of all those things which arouse the wrath of
God."[30]

Languidness in chanting is condemned by the Fathers. We have
just noted how St. Symeon counsels the canonarch not to chant
carelessly and lazily. St. Maximos the Confessor, addressing all
those who profess to love God, exhorts them to devote themselves
to psalmody and prayer without sloth.[31] And St. Ephraim the
Syrian (4th century) admonishes Christians: "Be not strong in dis-
putation and languid in psalmody."[32] But *forced* and *unduly loud*
chanting is also condemned. The 75th canon of the Synod in
Trullo says: "We will that those whose office it is to psalmodize
in the churches do not use disorderly vociferations, nor force
nature to shouting."

Jeremiah of Sinai (18th century), in his paraphrase of the
Ladder of St. John Climacos, stresses the need of *preserving the
right tempo,* psalmodizing neither faster nor slower than is
proper.[33] He also stresses the need of *rendering every verse "in-
tegrally and perfectly."*[34] Since the melody and rhythm of a psalm
or ode emphasize and enhance the meaning of the words, and the
words give the rhythm and melody specific, definite content, it is
important that *both* be rendered properly. Every verse, every phrase,
every word must be sung in such a way that the meaning of the
text is not obscured or altered. Breathing at the wrong time, dividing the verses at the wrong places, wrong emphasis — these must

all be avoided. This is important, when we recall Paul's words, which are reiterated by the Fathers, to *"teach* and *admonish* one another with psalms and hymns and spiritual songs."

Historians of Byzantine music are agreed that Byzantine sacred music was from the very beginning *wholly vocal,* not at all instrumental. Among them, H. J. W. Tillyard observes that "Byzantine music was vocal and was sung by a professional cantor or by a trained choir in unison. No instruments were used in the Greek Church."[35] And Egon Wellesz remarks: "Byzantine ecclesiastical music was entirely vocal. . . . The use of organs and other instruments was forbidden inside the churches."[36]

The *execution* of Byzantine church music by *instruments,* or *even the accompaniment* of sacred chanting by *instruments, was ruled out by the Eastern Fathers* as being incompatible with the pure, solemn, spiritual character of the religion of Christ. "The Fathers of the Church," observes G. I. Papadopoulos, "in accordance with the example of the psalmodizing of our Savior and the holy Apostles, established that only vocal music be used in the churches and severely forbade instrumental music as being secular and hedonic, and in general as evoking pleasure without spiritual value."[37] And Chrysostom, commenting on the verse: "O God, I will sing a new song to Thee; I will play to Thee on a psaltery of ten strings," of psalm 143, says: "That is, I shall give thanks to Thee. But then there were musical instruments through which they executed their sacred songs; but now, instead of instruments we employ the body."[39] And later, commenting on Psalm 150, he says: "God at that time permitted them [the Jews] to use instruments on account of their weakness. . . . For in His wisdom He devised to awaken them in this way from their gross, sluggish, and despondent state."[40] The point is that thanks to the coming of Christ with His message of a *New* Man and a *New* Earth, Christians are in a more favorable position than those that lived under the Old Covenant, and hence *more is demanded of them* — they are expected to rise to a *higher* spiritual level.

The use of the organ in the Western Church, which started in the Middle Ages, and the imitation of this practice by certain Orthodox churches in the West in our time, is clearly contrary to the practice of the early Christians and the teaching of the Greek Fathers.

In the performance of Byzantine sacred music, not only are all musical instruments excluded, but also *polyphony* (or *hetero-phony*). As was indicated at the beginning, Byzantine sacred music is *monophonic* (or *homophonic*).[41] This means that there is only *one* part, so that even when many chanters take part in the psalmody, they all chant together, "as though their voices were coming out of one mouth," as Chrysostom puts it.[42]

On this point, historians of Byzantine music are again in agreement. Tillyard says that Byzantine music "is vocal, *in one part,* without accompaniment other than the drone or holding-note."[43] And Wellesz asserts that "Byzantine ecclesiastical music ... whether chanted by one or more singers or by a choir, was always homophonic."[44] Similarly D. G. Panagiotopoulos observes that "Byzantine melody, holding the very ancient tradition, ... always proceeds on one line of sounds and does not employ a harmony in various tones, as is done in the case of European music. Hence, even when many chant together, they chant exactly the same sounds — there are not different lines of melody, with different tones."[45]

It is worth noting in this connection, that even in Western Christendom sacred music was entirely monophonic during the first ten centuries.[46] Polyphony, or the "harmonization," as it is called, of Byzantine chant according to Western principles of harmony and counterpoint, like its implementation by organ accompaniment is, then, contrary to the tradition of the Christian Church. It is an innovation which was introduced into Russian churches in the eighteenth century, and later into other Orthodox churches. This innovation is a result of Western influence upon the East; for the Western Church introduced polyphonic singing at a much earlier date.

This innovation, which assumes the form of singing in harmony by two or more voices, radically changes the outer form of Byzantine sacred music, and thereby its inner essence also. It destroys its pureness and sublimity, its mystical quality, its power of evoking contrition, and transforms it into something which is rather a means of pleasure and entertainment. Byzantine melodies, when clothed with harmonic parts, lose their distinctive expressiveness, their spiritual rhythm, their spiritual grandeur, and thereby their power of uplifting and transforming us spiritually.[47]

Monophonic chanting is not only the chanting that is in accord with the practice of the ancient Christian Church, but also the one that is truly in accord with the simple, humble, serious character of Christ and His teaching. For polyphony introduces an element of undue complexity, as well as of ostentation and lightness.

In order to enrich and augment the melody, Byzantine sacred music employs, instead of polyphony and the accompaniment of the organ or some other instrument, a finer, more spiritual means: the *isocratēma* or *holding-note*. That is, in addition to the chanters (*psaltai*), who sing the melody, there are the *isocrats* (literally, "holders of the *ison*" or fundamental tone) or, as they are named in ancient Byzantine manuscripts, *bastaktai* (literally, "holders"). The work of the isocrats consists in holding a drone on the basic tone of the mode in which the melody is being sung.

The isocratema is executed by one or more voices, usually in the lower finalis or key-note. Sometimes it is sung simultaneously in the higher finalis by boys.[48] It commences at the same time as the melody, or a little before it, as soon as the cantor gives the ison. The loudness of the isocratema does not remain the same throughout the execution of a hymn, but varies according to the loudness with which the melody is sung.

The isocratema not only enhances the melody, but also emphasizes the mode in which the psalm, hymn or ode is being sung, and adds solemnness and power to the psalmody. Its use goes back to the early Christian period.[49]

In order to provide the chanters with needed periods of rest, and to keep the congregation in a state of inner wakefulness, so necessary in Christian life, especially during worship, *antiphony* is employed in Byzantine chant. That is, not one but two choirs are employed, which psalmodize alternately. In this way, the chanter or chanters of one choir can rest while the other chanter or chanters psalmodize, and the congregation are not subjected to the sleep-conducive monotony of hearing continuously the same voice or

Α— μην ευ λο γει η ψυ χη μου τον Κυ ρι ον ευ λο

γη τος ει Κυ ρι ε ευ λο ο ο γει ει η ψυ χη μου τον

Κυ υ ρι ον q και παντα τα τα εν το ος μου το ο νο μα το

α γι ον αυ του

Ε υ λο γει η ψυ χη μου τον Κυ ρι ον και μη ε πι λαν θα νου

πα σας τας αν τα πο δο σεις αυ του

Τ ον ευ ι λα τευ ον τα πα σας τας α νο μι ι ας σου τον

ι ω με νον πα σας τας νο σους σου

19.   Byzantine music has its own system of musical scales, its own laws and canons, its own modes of composition, its own system of notation. Above is an excerpt from a composition by Petros the Peloponnesian (18th century), one of the most remarkable cantors and composers of Byzantine chant after the fall of Constantinople. It is written in the reformed Byzantine notation, developed by Chrysanthos (d. 1843), Gregory (d. 1822), and Hourmouzios (d. 1840). The symbols above the words are interval signs. They do not give the pitch of every tone in the melody, but indicate how many tones a certain note lies above or below the preceding one, or whether it is a repetition of it.

Mode IV Plagal (Finalis C).

20. The above is a transcription of the composition shown on the preceding page. (*Courtesy Holy Transfiguration Monastery, Boston.*)

voices, coming from the same part of the church.

The practice of antiphonal chanting can be traced as far back as the time of the Apostolic Fathers. Ancient writers, such as the Church historian Socrates, who wrote during the fifth century, say that the first one to introduce antiphonal chanting into the Church was Ignatios, bishop of Antioch.[50] This important Apostolic Father lived from about the middle of the first century to the early part of the second. In the fourth century, antiphonal psalmodizing was used in Egypt, Libya, Palestine, Arabia, Phoenicia, Syria, Mesopotamia, and elsewhere.[51]

From what has been said regarding the inner, spiritual state necessary for rendering Byzantine sacred music properly, it is clear that the chanter must be a true Christian, possessing real piety, humility, inner wakefulness, and understanding — an understanding not only of what he is chanting, but also of the important purpose which he has been appointed to serve. Needless to say, he must also have a superior voice and musical sensibility, and must have received an adequate training in chanting Byzantine music.

These things were realized by the Fathers of the Church from the earliest period. In the Apostolic Canons, in the canons of the Synod of Laodicea and of the Synod in Trullo, chanters are classified among the clergy (*klēros*),[52] and a stricter mode of life is required of them than of laymen.[53] Further, the Synod of Laodicea established that "No others shall psalmodize in church, except the canonical chanters."[54]

CHAPTER TEN

HYMNODY

Byzantine hymnody, which constitutes the largest and most important part of medieval Greek poetry, is one of the most precious treasures of the Greek Orthodox Church. This hymnody is distinguished into two kinds, the liturgical and the merely religious. Of these, the first is the more important. Liturgical hymnody consists of hymns that are intended to be sung in church, and is employed in all the services. The poetry here conforms to sacred melodies. The merely religious hymns, on the other hand, are intended simply to be read. Both of these kinds of poetry are original in form as well as in content. St. Romanos the Melodist (5th-6th centuries) and St. John of Damascus are the greatest composers of liturgical hymns, while St. Gregory Nazianzen and St. Symeon the New Theologian are among the most important writers of non-liturgical hymns. But there have been numerous other hymnographers, whose works are of great merit, both as poetry and as theology or "sacred philosophy."

We shall concern ourselves here with the liturgical hymnody alone. This is contained in six liturgical collections making up seventeen large volumes: the *Paraklētikē* or *Great Octōēchos*, the *Triōdion*, the *Pentēkostarion*, the *Mēnaia*, the *Hōrologion*, and the *Great Euchologion*.

The *Paraklētikē* contains chiefly hymns commemorating the Resurrection of Christ, together with canons addressed to the Holy Trinity. The canon is the most elaborate type of hymn, generally consisting of eight odes, and sometimes of nine. This book is divided into the eight modes or tones (*ēchoi*) of Byzantine music: the First, Second, Third, and Fourth "Authentic" (*Kyrioi*) Modes, and the First, Second, Third (or *Barys,* "Grave"), and Fourth "Plagal" (*Plagioi*) Modes. Each week, the hymns in one of these

modes are chanted. Commencing with the hymns in the First Mode
on the Sunday after the Sunday of all Saints, the hymns in the
Second Mode are chanted during the next week, those in the Third
Mode are sung during the following week, and so on, until those of
the Plagal of the Fourth Mode, which is the eighth Mode, have
been sung. Then the cycle of the eight modes is repeated during
the next eight weeks; and so on, until the Sunday of the Publican
and the Pharisee, when the period of the *Triōdion* begins.

In the *Triōdion* are included the services for the Great Lent
and the four weeks that precede it. The hymns in this book have
reference to various events in the Old and the New Testaments,
but especially to the Passion of Jesus.

The *Pentēkostarion* contains the Easter Day service and the
services for all the subsequent movable holy days until the Sunday
of All Saints — the Sunday after Pentecost.

The *Mēnaia* are twelve volumes, one for each month of the
year. In the Eastern Church, each day of the month has a special
vesper service (*hesperinos*) and matins (*orthros*), containing hymns
for the saint or saints commemorated on that day; and hence each
volume of this collection is divided into as many parts as the particular month for which it has been composed has days.

In the *Hōrologion* are contained chiefly the *apolytikia* and
kontakia for all the holy days of the year, and certain *akolouthias*
or services such as the *Akathistos Hymn,* the canons of entreaty to
the Theotokos or Holy Virgin Mary, etc. An *apolytikion* is a short
hymn chanted towards the end of a service and having reference
to the sacred person or event commemorated on the particular day
when it is sung, while a *kontakion* is a short hymn which sums up
the life of a saint or expresses the main point of the occasion for
which it is used. The *Akathistos Hymn* is a special *akolouthia,*
dating from the 6th century, dedicated to the Theotokos and held
on the first five Fridays of the Great Lent.

Finally, the *Great Euchologion* comprises the liturgies of St.
Chrysostom and St. Basil, the services for the Mysteries or "Sacra-
ments," Burial, etc.

The language in which Byzantine liturgical hymns are written
is the ancient Greek, although often in a fairly simplified form.

But this poetry owes little to classical models.[1] What it has in common with the latter, besides the Greek language, is chiefly clarity, simplicity, and restraint — qualities that characterize Greek genius. These hymns are distinguished by *free rhythm* and, generally, by a *lack of rhyme*. Measured rhythm or meter, which Westerners expect to find in hymns, is not to be found in these. Rhyme is employed only occasionally, particularly for the purpose of emphasizing a connection between certain thoughts. The form of the language of these hymns can best be characterized as *cadenced poetic prose*.[2] There are exceptions, such as certain hymns of St. John Damascene, which are in iambics.

In its inner essence, Byzantine hymnody is identical with Byzantine music, architecture, and iconography. It differs from them only in employing a different medium: language. Like them it seeks to introduce us to a realm of being that lies beyond the world which is apprehended by the senses, to lift us to a higher level of experience, to the level of spiritual beauty, of holiness, of the Divine.

The themes of the hymnographer are the Holy Trinity, Christ, the Theotokos, the Prophets, the Apostles, the Martyrs, the Church Fathers and the rest of the Saints, and in some instances the Archangels. They are the power, wisdom, justice, mercy, beauty and other attributes of God; the life, teaching, and miracles of Christ; the life and virtues of the Theotokos and of the Saints. These themes are treated *objectively*, without the poet injecting into them either his idiosyncrasy or matters pertaining to his own individual life. This point is brought out with great clarity and emphasis by John Brownlie in his book *Hymns of the Greek Church*. "One prime characteristic of Greek hymnody," he remarks, "should be referred to. Unlike our English hymn which is intensely subjective — in many cases unhealthily so — the Greek hymn is in most cases objective. God, in the glory of His majesty, and clothed with His attributes, is held up to the worship and adoration of His people. Christ in His person and work is set before the mind in a most realistic manner. His birth and its accompaniments; His life; the words He spoke and the works He did; His passion in all the agony of its detail; the denial of Peter; the remorse of Judas; the

Crucifixion; the darkness, the terror, the opened graves; the penitent thief, the loud cry, the death; — all are depicted in plain unmistakable language. So we have in the hymns of the Greek Church a pictorial representation of the history of Redemption which, by engaging the mind, appeals ultimately to the heart and its emotions."[3]

It is not his ego or his place and time that the hymnographer seeks to express, but the facts, truths, and values of Christian religion, and the feelings that it is proper for a devout Christian to express, such as praise of God and of the Saints, gratitude to them, entreaty, hope and love.

Thus, the following Resurrectional Apolytikion of the Fourth Mode expresses the event described in Luke 24:1-10:

> "The women disciples of the Lord, having learned from the Angel the joyous proclamation of the Resurrection, and the abolition of the ancestral sentence, with exultation announced to the Apostles: Death is despoiled, Christ our God has arisen, and gives to the world the Great Mercy."[4]

The Resurrectional Apolytikion of the First Plagal Mode is a hymn of praise to Christ:

> "Let us, the faithful, praise and worship the Logos, co-eternal with the Father and the Spirit, and for our salvation born of a Virgin; for He willed to be lifted upon the Cross in the flesh, and to endure death, and to raise the dead by His glorious Resurrection."[5]

Feelings of praise are also conveyed by the following *Martyrikon*, or hymn addressed to the Martyrs:

> "Let all peoples honor with hymns and spiritual odes the Victorious Martyrs of Christ, the luminaries of the world and heralds of the Faith, the eternal fount from which there gush up cures for the faithful."[6]

Often such hymns end as exhortations to the faithful to imitate the virtues and deeds of the Saint or Saints.

In the following hymn, which is sung on Easter, the feeling of hope finds vivid expression:

> "Oh, how divine, how beloved, how superla-
> tively sweet is Thy voice! Because Thou hast
> promised us, O Christ, that Thou wilt be
> with us until the end of time. And we, hold-
> ing onto Thy words as to an anchor of hope,
> are glad and rejoice."[7]

Frequently, hymns are entreaties addressed to God asking for aid whereby the faithful may overcome temptations, become truthful, courageous, meek, blameless, pure, sharers of God's wisdom and blessedness. The following hymn, which is sung in the *orthros* of the Sunday of the Publican and the Pharisee, is an example:

> "O Thou Giver-of-life, open for me the gates
> of repentance; for my spirit, entirely defiled,
> bearing the temple of the body, chants the
> morning office before Thy temple. But Thou,
> being merciful, cleanse me through Thy
> compassionate mercy."[8]

Hymns of entreaty are often addressed to the Theotokos, the Apostles, and other Saints, as intercessors to God. It is a belief, deeply rooted in the Orthodox consciousness, that the Saints, who when on earth prayed for their brethren, continue to intercede for them to the Lord after their death, as members of the triumphant Church of Christ in Heaven. This belief finds vivid expression in Byzantine hymnody. Thus, the hymn that immediately follows the one just quoted is addressed to the Holy Virgin and says:

> "Make straight for me the paths of salvation,
> O Theotokos; for I have defiled my soul with
> ugly sins, having spent my whole life in a
> state of inner sleep. Through thy interces-
> sions deliver me from every impurity."[9]

The same type of entreaty is expressed in the following hymn to the Apostles:

> "Apostles who have seen God, illumine my
> soul, which is darkened by passions — you
> who through your divine teachings have
> illumined the world and diminished the dark-
> ness of the idols. And now intercede that
> peace and the Great Mercy be given to
> our souls."[10]

The concern for the beautiful is of the essence of Byzantine hymnody. But the beauty that concerns it is the spiritual, not the physical. The latter is brought into the hymns only by way of comparison, as a means of expressing the beauty that is spiritual. "Our whole Ecclesiastical hymnography," remarks a contemporary Greek theologian, Theokletos Dionysiatis, "is adorned with words denoting beauty — *kallos, hōraiotēs, hōraios, kallonē* — but their meaning is entirely spiritual. Often there is made use in it of beautiful aesthetic images from the earthly, as rather weak means of comparison, for indicating divine spiritual beauty."[11] The concern is for the beauty of the Holy Trinity, of the Divine Logos — Christ — of the mind, of the soul, of the virtues. At every oppor- tunity the hymnographers extol the beauty of the Divine nature, of the uncreated Divine light, of the blessed Angels and Saints, who mirror the Divine Beauty by their possession of piety, purity, love, and other similar qualities. They seek thereby not only to praise God and His holy followers in a worthy manner, but also to arouse the worshippers spiritually, to incite them to apply them- selves with greater energy to the urgent task of transforming their inner being. Characteristic in this regard are the following hymns, in which God is viewed as the supreme, ineffable Beauty, that is the ultimate source of beauty of the soul:

> "Thou wast transfigured on the Mountain, O
> Christ our God, having shown to Thy dis-
> ciples Thy glory as they were able to behold
> it. Shine upon us sinners, too, Thy light

eternal, through the intercessions of the Theotokos. O Giver-of-light, glory to Thee."[12]

"Thou hast created the incorporeal and heavenly Angelic Hosts as mirrors of Thy
beauty, O indivisible Trinity, Sole Ruler, to
sing unceasingly to Thee. And now accept
from our earthen lips our hymn of praise."[13]

"Make straight the hearts of Thy servants
towards the unapproachable light, O Thrice
resplendent Lord, and bestow the effulgence
of Thy glory upon our souls, that we may
behold Thy ineffable beauty."[14]

NOTES

Chapter One

Philosophy

1. B. Tatakis, *La Philosophie byzantine,* Paris, Presses Universitaires, 1949, p. v.
2. *Ibid.*
3. *Ibid.,* p. 72.
4. *Ibid.,* pp. 3, 123.
5. *Ibid.,* p. v.
6. *Ibid.,* p. 7.
7. *Ibid.,* p. 106. The italics are mine.
8. *Ibid.,* p. 271. The italics are mine.
9. *Ibid.,* p. 287.
10. *Ibid.,* p. 288.
11. Migne, *Patrologia Graeca,* Vol. 6, col. 464. Henceforth I shall refer to this series as *P.G.*
12. *P.G.,* Vol. 6, col. 492.
13. *Ibid.,* col. 460.
14. *Ibid.,* col. 381.
15. See *The Ante-Nicene Fathers,* Vol. 9, New York, 1896, p. 259.
16. Eusebius of Caesarea, *Ecclesiastical History and The Martyrs of Palestine,* trans. by H. J. Lawlor and J. E. L. Oulton, Vol. 2, London, 1928, p. 192.
17. *Ibid,* Vol. 1, 1927, pp. 353, 389; Vol. 2, p. 332.
18. *Stromateis,* Bk. VI, Ch. 7. Here and elsewhere in this chapter I have used the translation of William Wilson, *The Writings of Clement of Alexandria,* in *Ante-Nicene Christian Library,* Edinburgh, 1867.
19. *Philokalia,* Athens, 1893, Vol. 1, p. 111.
20. Cf. Athanasios Parios, *Epitomē, eite Syllogē tōn Theiōn*

tēs Pisteōs Dogmatōn, "Epitome, or Collection of the Divine Dogmas of the Faith," Leipzig, 1806, pp. 1-2.

21. Arthur J. Mason, ed., *The Five Theological Orations of Gregory of Nazianzus,* Cambridge, 1899, pp. xv-xvi.

22. This poem constitutes Part II of the monumental book *Tou Hosiou Symeōn tou Neou Theologou ta Heuriskomena,* "The Extant Works of Saint Symeon the New Theologian," ed. by Dionysios Zagoraios, Syros, 1886.

23. *Philokalia,* Vol. 1, pp. 111-112.

24. *Ibid.,* Vol. 2, p. 260.

25. *P.G.,* Vol. 150, col. 668.

26. *Klimax,* "The Ladder," Constantinople, 1883, p. 155.

27. *Ibid.*

28. *Ibid.,* p. 156.

29. *Philokalia,* Vol. 1, p. 97.

30. *Ibid.,* pp. 92-93.

31. *Ibid.,* Vol. 2, p. 399.

32. *Pēgē Gnōseōs,* in *P.G.,* Vol. 94, col. 669.

33. *Philokalia,* Vol. 2, p. 260.

34. Eusebius, *The Proof of the Gospel,* ed. by W. J. Ferrar, London and New York, 1920, Vol. 1, p. 48.

35. See e.g. Eusebius, *Ecclesiastical History,* Bk. II, Ch. 17, Bk. VI, Ch. 9, and Chrysostom, *P.G.* Vol. 49, cols. 189-190. Cf. F. J. A. Hort, *Judaistic Christianity,* Cambridge and London, 1894, p. 121, and J. H. Srawley, ed., *The Catechetical Oration of Gregory of Nyssa,* Cambridge, 1903, p. 76.

36. *P.G.,* Vol. 35, col. 1204.

37. *Ibid.,* col. 765.

38. *Stromateis,* Bk. I, Ch. 5.

39. *Ibid.*

40. *Ibid.,* Bk. VI, Ch. 8.

41. *Ibid.,* Bk. I, Ch. 5; cf. Ch. 13.

42. *Ibid.,* Ch. 7.

43. *Ibid.,* Ch. 3.

44. *Ibid.,* Bk. VI, Ch. 8.

45. *Ibid.,* Bk. I, Ch. 11.

46. *Ibid.,* Bk. VI, Ch. 11.

47. *Address to Young Men on the Right Use of Greek Litera-ture,* in *Essays on the Study and Use of Poetry by Plutarch and Basil the Great,* trans. by Frederick M. Padelford, New York, 1902, pp. 101, 102.

48. *Ibid.,* p. 103.

49. *Ibid.*

50. *Ibid.,* p. 120.

51. *Ibid.,* p. 107.

52. *Ibid.,* p. 106.

53. *Ibid.,* p. 110.

54. *Ibid.,* p. 105.

55. *Ibid.,* p. 104.

56. *Exposition of the Orthodox Faith,* Bk. IV, Ch. 17, in *A Select Library of the Nicene and Post-Nicene Fathers,* Second Series, Vol. 9, New York, 1899. Henceforth I shall refer to this library as *Nicene and Post-Nicene Fathers.*

57. *P.G.,* Vol. 150, col. 588.

58. Eph. 6: 12.

59. *The Extant Works of Saint Symeon the New Theologian,* Part I, p. 527.

60. *P.G.,* Vol. 3, col. 373.

61. *Spiritual Homilies,* XXX.

62. *Op..cit.,* Part II, p. 24.

63. *Philokalia,* Vol. 2, p. 210.

CHAPTER TWO

The Way to Knowledge

1. *The Extant Works of Saint Symeon the New Theologian,* Part I, p. 88.

2. *Philokalia,* Vol. 1, p. 60.

3. *The Ladder,* p. 149.

4. *Philokalia,* Vol. 1, p. 340.

5. *Ibid.,* Vol. 2, p. 178.

6. *Op. cit.,* Part I, p. 527.

7. *Philokalia,* Vol. 1, pp. 233-234.

8. *Ibid.,* p. 59.

9. *Ibid.,* p. 67.

10. *Op. cit.,* Part I, p. 103.

11. *Philokalia,* Vol. 1, p. 88.

12. *Ibid.,* Vol. 2, p. 195.

13. *Abba Isaia Logoi Eikosiennaia,* "Twenty-nine Discourses by Abba Isaiah," Volos, 1962, p. 167.

14. *Op. cit.,* Part I, p. 114.

15. *Op. cit.,* p. 169.

16. *Philokalia,* Vol. 1, p. 339.

17. *Ibid.,* p. 202.

18. *Ibid.,* p. 203.

19. *Ibid.,* Vol. 2, p. 15.

20. *Ibid.,* Vol. 1, p. 348.

21. *The Extant Works of St. Symeon the New Theologian,* Introduction, p. 25.

22. *Symeon Archiepiskopou Thessalonikēs ta Hapanta,* "The Collected Works of Symeon Archbishop of Thessaloniki," 4th ed., Athens, 1882, p. 316.

23. *Philokalia,* Vol. 1, p. 338.

24. *Ibid.,* p. 340.

25. *Ibid.,* p. 349.

26. *Ibid.,* p. 230.

27. E.g. by Palladios (*P.G.,* Vol. 34, cols. 1012, 1017) and Thalassios (*Philokalia,* Vol. 1, p. 330).

28. E.g. by Mark the Ascetic (*Philokalia,* Vol. 1, p. 62).

29. Abba Dorotheos, *P.G.,* Vol. 88, col. 1653.

30. *A Select Library of the Nicene and Post-Nicene Fathers,* Second Series, New York, 1892, Vol. 4, p. 22.

31. *P.G.,* Vol. 44, col. 184.

32. *Ibid.,* Vol. 120, cols. 957, 960. Cf. St. Macarios the Egyptian: "The heart has many natural thoughts joined to it. . . . These pure, natural thoughts were created by God" (*P.G.,* Vol. 34, cols. 593, 600).

33. *Philokalia,* Vol. 2, pp. 104-105.

34. *Ibid.,* Vol. 1, p. 195.

35. *Ibid.*

36. *Ibid.,* p. 100.

37. *Ibid.,* p. 256.

38. In Chapter Three.

39. *Philokalia,* Vol. 2, p. 243.

40. *Ibid.,* Vol. 1, p. 13.

41. *Ibid.,* Vol. 2, p. 86.

Chapter Three

Conscience

1. Tit. 1: 15.

2. 1 Tim. 1: 5.

3. 2 Cor. 1: 12.

4. 24: 16.

5. 8: 9.

6. 1 Peter 3: 21.

7. *P.G.,* Vol. 88, col. 1652.

8. *Philokalia,* Vol. 1, p. 223.

9. *The Ladder,* p. 124.

10. *Nicene and Post-Nicene Fathers,* First Series, Vol. 13, New York, 1889, p. 494.

11. *Op. cit.,* p. 80.

12. *Ibid.,* p. 58.

13. *Philokalia,* Vol. 1, p. 330.

14. *Nicene and Post-Nicene Fathers,* First Series, Vol. 11, p. 342.

15. *Symbouleutikon Encheiridion,* "Handbook of Counsel," Vienna, 1801, p. 186.

16. *Philokalia,* Vol. 1, p. 94.

17. *P.G.,* Vol. 88, col. 1653.

18. Matt. 5: 25.

19. *Op. cit.,* col. 1653.

20. *Spiritual Homilies,* XV.

21. *Nicene and Post-Nicene Fathers,* First Series, Vol. 9, p. 451.

22. *Ibid.,* Vol. 10, p. 253.

23. Venice, 1876, p. 263.
24. Venice, 1851, p. 119.
25. *The Ladder*, p. 36.
26. *Philokalia*, Vol. 1, p. 330.
27. *Spiritual Homilies*, XV.
28. *Ibid.*
29. *P.G.*, Vol. 63, col. 81.
30. *The Ladder*, p. 62.
31. *Ibid.*, p. 67.
32. *Philokalia*, Vol. 2, p. 196.
33. *Nicene and Post-Nicene Fathers*, First Series, Vol. 12, p. 314.
34. P. 78.
35. *P.G.*, Vol. 88, col. 1653.
36. *Ibid.*
37. *Philokalia*, Vol. 1, p. 18.
38. *P.G.*, Vol. 88, cols. 1653, 1656.
39. *Philokalia*, Vol. 1, p. 18.
40. *Ibid.*, p. 371.
41. *Ibid.*, p. 63.
42. *Ibid.*, p. 180.
43. *Ibid.*, p. 66.
44. *Ibid.*, Vol. 2, p. 306.

CHAPTER FOUR

The *Philokalia*

1. By Astir Publishing Company of Al. and E. Papademe-triou. Since this was written, the publication of the series has been completed.
2. *Philokalia*, Vol. 1, p. 346.
3. *Ibid.*
4. Vol. 1, p. 141.
5. Vol. 2, p. 322.
6. Vol. 2, p. 281.
7. Vol. 2, p. 243.
8. Vol. 2, p. 4.
9. Vol. 1, p. 195.

10. Vol. 1, p. 62.
11. Vol. 2, p. 272.
12. Vol. 2, p. 516.
13. Vol. 2, p. 434.
14. Vol. 2, p. 12.
15. Vol. 2, p. 168.
16. Vol. 2, p. 151.
17. Vol. 2, p. 231.
18. Vol. 2, p. 384.
19. Vol. 2, p. 396.
20. Vol. 2, p. 323.
21. Vol. 2, p. 399.
22. Vol. 1, p. 25.
23. Vol. 2, p. 240.
24. Vol. 2, pp. 512-513.

CHAPTER FIVE

Aesthetic Examination of Byzantine Art

1. London, Batsford, 1955. In writing this paper in 1952 I made use of the original Greek edition, entitled *Aisthētikē Theōrēsē tēs Byzantinēs Technēs* (Athens, 1946).

2. Cf. Santayana, *The Sense of Beauty*, New York, 1896, p. 109, where he refers to Byzantine architecture as "vague and barbarous" compared with classical Greek architecture. Herbert Read expresses the opinion that "it is Gibbon, with his inability to appreciate Christian values, who more than anyone else has retarded the true appreciation of Byzantine art" (*The Meaning of Art*, New York, 1951, pp. 116-117).

3. Cf. Read: "Byzantine art . . . is the purest form of religious art that Christianity has experienced" (*op. cit.*, p. 117).

4. For an extensive treatment of the subject see my study "Iconographic Decoration in the Orthodox Church," in *The Orthodox Ethos,* ed. by A. J. Philippou, Oxford, 1964.

CHAPTER SIX

Iconography

1. Athens, Astir Publishing Co., Al. and E. Papademetriou.
2. Leo Tolstoy, *What is Art? And Essays on Art*, trans. by A. Maude, Oxford, 1929, p. 179.
3. *Ibid.*, p. 178.

CHAPTER SEVEN

Manuel Panselinos

1. The *iconostasis* is a wooden or marble screen, or a wall, supporting panel icons and separating the sanctuary (*bēma*) from the main body of the church. In the Church of the Protaton the iconostasis is made of marble.
2. *Hermēneia tēs Zōgraphikēs Technēs,* ed. by A. Papa-dopolous-Kerameus, Petroupolis (Petrograd), 1909, p. 3.

CHAPTER EIGHT

El Greco and Byzantine Art

1. New York, The Macmillan Co.
2. *Op. cit.,* p. ix.
3. *Ibid.,* p. x.
4. *Ibid.,* p. 3.
5. *Ibid.,* p. 8.
6. *Ibid.,* p. 2.
7. *Ibid.,* p. 8.
8. *Ibid.,* pp. 158a-158b.
9. *Ibid.,* p. 114.
10. *Ibid.,* p. 112.
11. Pope Gregory the Great.
12. *Op. cit.,* p. 113.
13. *Ibid.*

CHAPTER NINE

Sacred Music

1. Matthew 26: 30; Mark 14: 26.
2. 19: 37-38.
3. 5: 19.
4. 3: 16.
5. 2: 12.
6. 16: 25.
7. 5: 18-19.
8. 3: 16.
9. 2.
10. *The Extant Works of Saint Symeon the New Theologian,* Part I, pp. 60, 102, 145.
11. John 1: 12.
12. Gal. 4: 7.
13. *P.G.,* Vol. 94, cols. 1164, 1165, 1168.
14. *P.G.,* Vol. 27, col. 40.
15. *Ibid.,* cols. 40-41.
16. 2.
17. 207.
18. *P.G.,* Vol. 55, col. 156.
19. *P.G.,* Vol. 62, col. 129.
20. *Philokalia,* Vol. 1, p. 34.
21. *Ibid.,* p. 49.
22. *Ibid.,* p. 107.
23. *P.G.,* Vol. 88, col. 832.
24. *Ibid.,* col. 680.
25. *Ibid.,* col. 861.
26. *Ibid.,* col. 1137.
27. *P.G.,* Vol. 62, col. 364.
28. *The Extant Works of Saint Symeon the New Theologian,* Part I, p. 61.
29. *Ibid.,* p. 373.
30. *Ibid.,* p. 102.
31. *Philokalia,* Vol. 1, p. 204.
32. *Ta tou Hosiou Patros hēmōn Ephraim tou Syrou Askētika,*

"The Ascetic Works of our Holy Father Ephraim the Syrian," trans. by Markos D. Sakorraphos, Athens, 1864, p. 69.

33. *Nea Klimax,* "New Ladder," ed. by Soterios N. Schoinas, Volos, 1938, p. 236.

34. *Ibid.,* p. 173.

35. "Byzantine Music," in *Encyclopedia Britannica,* 1941, Vol. 4, p. 492.

36. *A History of Byzantine Music and Hymnography,* Oxford, 1949, p. 24.

37. *Historikē Episkopēsis tēs Byzantinēs Ekklēsiastikēs Mousikēs,* "A Historical Survey of Byzantine Ecclesiastical Music," Athens, 1904, pp. 10-11.

38. *P.G.,* Vol. 35, col. 709.

39. *P.G.,* Vol. 55, col. 462. Cf. Clement of Alexandria, P.G., Vol. 8, cols. 441, 444.

40. *P.G.,* Vol. 55, cols. 497-498.

41. Cf. *Gregorii Nysseni Opera Ascetica,* ed. by Werner Jaeger, Leiden, 1952, p. 408.

42. *P.G.,* Vol. 61, col. 315.

43. *Byzantine Music and Hymnography,* London, 1923, p. 37. The italics are mine.

44. *Op. cit.,* p. 24.

45. *Theōria kai Praxis tēs Byzantinēs Ekklēsiastikēs Mousikēs,* "The Theory and Practice of Byzantine Ecclesiastical Music," Athens, 1947, p. 285.

46. See e.g. *The New Schaff-Herzog Encyclopedia of Religious Knowledge,* Vol. 10, p. 157.

47. Cf. Panagiotopoulos, *op. cit.,* pp. 302, 342.

48. Cf. Tillyard, *Byzantine Music and Hymnography,* p. 64; Panagiotopoulos, *op. cit.,* p. 290.

49. See e.g. St. Basil's *Homily on Famine and Drought,* *P.G.,* Vol. 31, col. 309.

50. *P.G.,* Vol. 67, cols. 689, 692.

51. See Basil's Letter 207. Cf. Theodoretos, *P.G.,* Vol. 82, col. 1060.

52. Apostolic Canons 26, 43, 69; canon 24 of the Synod of Laodicea (4th century); canons 4 and 5 of the Synod in Trullo.

53.   Apostolic Canons 42, 43, 69; canon 24 of the Synod of Laodicea.

54.   Canon 15.

CHAPTER TEN

Hymnody

1.   Cf. Tillyard, *Byzantine Music and Hymnography,* p. 8.

2.   Cf. Tillyard, *op. cit.,* p. 10; Wellesz, *A History of Byzantine Music and Hymnography,* p. 5.

3.   *Op. cit.,* Paisley, 1902, pp. 67-68. Cf. Tillyard, *op. cit.,* p. 26.

4.   *Hōrologion,* under *"Apolytikia Anastasima tōn Octō Ēchōn."*

5.   *Ibid.*

6.   *Paraklētikē,* Venice, 1851, p. 17.

7.   *Pentēkostarion,* Athens, 1960, p. 5.

8.   *Triōdion,* Venice, 1876, p. 2.

9.   *Ibid.*

10.   *Paraklētikē,* p. 30.

11.   *Metaxy Ouranou kai Gēs,* "Between Heaven and Earth," Athens, 1956, pp. 38-39.

12.   Apolytikion sung on the Feast of the Transfiguration, August 6. Contained in the *Hōrologion.*

14.   *Ibid.,* p. 94.

13.   *Paraklētikē,* p. 51.

GLOSSARY

I. *Greek-English**

agapē (agápi) — love

aisthēsis (ésthisis) — awareness, consciousness

akathistos (akáthistos) — not seated (The Akathistos Hymn is so designated, because the congregation does not sit while it is chanted.)

akēdia (akidía) — mental or spiritual torpor, low spirits

akolouthia (akoloothía) — church service

aktistos (áktistos) — uncreated

alloiōsis (allíosis) — change, transformation

anaisthēsia (anesthisía) — insensibility, unconsciousness

apatheia (apáthia) — dispassion, passionlessness

---

*The following system has been used in transliterating words:

α — a	ν — n	αι — ai		
β — b	ξ — x	ει — ei		
γ — g	ο — o	οι — oi	Dipthongs	
δ — d	π — p	αυ — au		
ε — e	ρ — r	ευ — eu		
ζ — z	σ — s	ου — ou		
η — ē	τ — t			
θ — th	υ — y			
ι — i	φ — ph	Rough breathing (ʽ) — h		
κ — k	χ — ch			
λ — l	ψ — ps			
μ — m	ω — ō	γ before κ, γ, χ — n		

In parenthesis, after each transliterated word, I have given a modern Greek phonetic equivalent. As regards the parenthesized, modern Greek phonetic equivalents, the following points should be noted. Pronounce

a like a in arm
d like th in thus
e like e in end
i like i in ill
o like o in obey
oo like oo in look
th like th in thin

apokatastasis (apokatástasis) — restoration

apolytikion (apolitíkion) — dismissal hymn; more specifically, a short hymn chanted towards the end of a service and having reference to the sacred person or event commemorated on the particular day when it is sung

aprospatheia (aprospáthia) — non-attachment

askēsis (áskisis) — spiritual training, spiritual work

bēma (víma) — sanctuary, i.e. the eastern part of the church, containing the altar or holy table

boulēsis (voólisis) — will

charmolypē (harmolípi) — gladdening sorrow

dianoia (diánia) — mind, intellect, discursive reason

diorasis (diórasis) — insight

dynamis (dínamis) — faculty, power

ēchos (íhos) — mode, tone (musical)

eikonostasion (ikonostásion) — iconostasis

ellampsis (éllampsis) — effulgence

erōs (éros) — love

energeia (enérgia) — energy, operation

epiklēsis (epíklisis) — invocation

epistēmē (epistími) — knowledge, science

erēmikos bios (erimikós víos) — eremitical life, monastic life

ergasia (ergasía) — work

esō (éso) — internal

esōterikos (esoterikós) — internal

ēthos (íthos) — character

euchē (efhí) — prayer

eutrapelia (eftrapelía) — joking, wittiness

exō (éxo) — outside, external

exōterikos (exoterikós) — external

hamartia (amartía) — sin

hekousioi ponoi (ekoósii poni) — voluntary suffering

henōsis (énosis) — union

hesperinos (esperinós) — vesper service

hēsychia (isihía) — quiet, stillness

hexis (éxis) — habit, settled disposition of the soul

hōraios (oréos) — beautiful

hōraiotēs (oreótis) — beauty
hyper (ipér) — above
hyperphyēs (iperphiís) — supernal
hyper physin (ipér phísin) — above nature
hypnos (ípnos) — sleep
isocratēma (isocrátima) — holding-note
kallos (kállos) — beauty
kardiakē proseuchē (kardiakí prosefhí) — prayer of the heart
kardiakon anoigma (kardiakón ánigma) — opening of the heart
kata kosmon (katá kósmon) — according to the world, secular
katanyxis (katánixis) — contrition
kata physin gnōsis (katá phísin gnósis) — knowledge according to nature
katastasis (katástasis) — condition, state
kat' eikona (kat' ikóna) — in the image
kathara proseuchē (kathará prosefhí) — pure prayer
katharsis (kátharsis) — purification
kath' homoiōsin (kath' omíosin) — in the likeness
klēros (klíros) — clergy
kontakion (kontákion) — a short hymn which sums up the life of a saint or expresses the main point of the occasion for which it is used
kybernētēs (kivernítis) — governor
logikos (logikós) — rational
logismos (logismós) — a thought
logos (lógos) — rational faculty, reason, word
Martyrikon (martirikón) — a hymn addressed to the holy martyrs
meletē (meléti) — meditation
mesoteichon (mesótihon) — dividing wall
meteōrizesthai (meteorízesthe) — to wander about mentally
nēpsis (nípsis) — wakefulness, attention
Nēptikoi Pateres (niptikí patéres) — Wakeful Fathers
noera proseuchē (noerá prosefhí) — mental prayer
noētos (noitós) — intelligible, mental
nous (noos) — mind, reason, intuitive reason
orthros (órthros) — matins
ousia (oosía) — essence, substance

para physin (pará phísin) — contrary to nature
patēr (patír) — father, spiritual guide and teacher
pathos (páthos) — passion, bad thought or feeling, vice
phantasia (phantasía) — imagination, mental image
philia (philía) — friendship, love
philokalia (philokalía) — love of the beautiful
philosophia (philosophía) — love of wisdom, philosophy
phōtismos (photismós) — illumination
phragmos (phragmós) — barrier
phronēsis (phrónisis) — good sense, moral wisdom
phylakē (philakí) — a guarding
physikē gnōsis (phisikí gnósis) — natural, innate knowledge
physis (phísis) — nature
plagios (plágios) — "oblique," plagal
pneumatikos (pnevmatikós) — spiritual
praxis (práxis) — act, action, deed
propaideia (propedía) — preparatory education
prosbolē (prosvolí) — suggestion
prosochē (prosohí) — attention
psaltēs (psáltis) — chanter
psychē (psihí) — soul
sōma (sóma) — body
sophia (sophía) — wisdom
sōteria (sotería) — salvation
stephanos (stéphanos) — halo, crown, wreath
syndyasmos (sindiasmós) — identification
synagōgē (sinagogí) — concentration
syneidēsis (sinídisis) — conscience
syneidos (sinidós) — conscience
synkatathesis (sinkatáthesis) — consent
technē (téhni) — art
theios (thíos) — divine
thelēsis (thélisis) — will
theōria (theoría) — contemplation, vision
theōsis (théosis) — deification, union with God — participation in
    His perfection and blessedness through Grace
Theotokos (theotókos) — "She who gave birth to God" (to the

second person of the Trinity, Christ), the Holy Virgin Mary

thyrathen (thírathen) — external, secular

II. *English-Greek*

above nature — *hyper physin*

act, action — *praxis*

art — *technē*

attention — *prosochē, nēpsis*

barrier — *phragmos*

beautiful — *kalos, hōraios*

beauty — *kalon, kallos, hōraiotēs*

body — *sōma*

change — *alloiōsis*

chanter — *psaltēs*

character — *ēthos*

clergy — *klēros*

concentration — *synagōgē*

conscience — *syneidēsis, syneidos*

consciousness — *aisthēsis*

consent — *synkatathesis*

contemplation — *theōria*

contrition — *katanyxis*

conversation — *synomilia, dialexis*

deification — *theōsis*

discernment — *diakrēsis*

discursive reason — *dianoia*

dismissal hymn — *apolytikion*

dividing wall — *mesoteichon*

divine — *theios*

effulgence — *ellampsis*

eremitical life — *erēmikos bios*

essence — *ousia*

external philosophy — *exō philosophia, exōterikē philosophia, thyrathen philosophia*

faculty (of soul) — *dynamis*

form — *eidos*

gladdening sorrow — *charmolypē*
governor — *kybernētēs*
guarding — *phylakē*
habit — *hexis*
halo — *stephanos*
heart — *kardia*
hesychasm — *hēsychasmos*
holding-note — *isocratēma*
iconostasis — *eikonostasion*
identification — *syndyasmos*
illumination — *phōtismos*
image — *eikon*
imagination — *phantasia*
inner quiet — *hēsychia*
inner wakefulness — *nēpsis*
insensibility — *anaisthēsia*
insight — *diorasis*
internal philosophy — *esō philosophia, esōterikē philosophia*
in the image — *kat' eikona*
in the likeness — *kath' homoiōsin*
intuitive reason — *nous*
Jesus Prayer — *euchē Iēsou, epiklēsis Iēsou*
knowledge — *epistēmē, gnōsis*
knowledge according to nature — *kata physin gnōsis*
love — *agapē, erōs, philia*
matins — *orthros*
meditation — *meletē*
mental — *noeros, noētos*
mental prayer — *noera proseuchē*
mind — *nous, dianoia*
mode (musical) — *ēchos*
natural knowledge — *physikē gnōsis*
nature — *physis*
non-attachment — *aprospatheia*
operation — *energeia*
passion — *pathos*
passionlessness — *apatheia*

philosophy — *philosophia*
plagal — *plagios*
prayer — *euchē, proseuchē*
prayer of the heart — *kardıakē proseuchē*
preparatory education — *propaideia*
psalmody — *psalmodia*
pure prayer — *kathara proseuchē*
purification — *katharsis*
rational — *logikos*
reason (faculty of) — *nous, logistikon, logos, dianoia*
restoration — *apokatastasis*
salvation — *sōtēria*
science — *epistēmē*
secular philosophy — *kata kosmon philosophia*
settled disposition of the soul — *hexis*
sin — *hamartia*
sleep — *hypnos*
soul — *psychē*
spiritual — *pneumatikos, noeros*
spiritual philosophy — *pneumatikē philosophia*
spiritual torpor — *akēdia*
spiritual training — *askēsis*
substance — *ousia*
suggestion — *prosbolē, hypobolē*
supernal — *hyperphyēs*
thoughts — *logismoi*
unconsciousness — *anaisthēsia*
uncreated energy — *aktistos energeia*
union — *henōsis*
vesper service — *hesperinos*
vision — *horama, horasis, optasia, theōria*
voluntary suffering — *hekousioi ponoi*
Wakeful Fathers — *Nēptikoi Pateres*
wandering (mental) — *meteōrismos, rembasmos*
will — *boulēsis, thelēsis, thelēma*
work — *ergasia*
world — *kosmos*

INDEX

Aidesios, 17
Akathistos Hymn, 110, 127
Akindynos, 15
Alexandria, 17, 22
Ammonios Saccas, 17
antiphony, 105, 108
Antony the Great, St., 39
apokatastasis, 29, 128
Apologists, 17
apolytikion, 110, 128
Apostolic Fathers, 108
architecture, 59, 63-4, 70, 72, 77, 78, 79, 110
Aristides, 17
Aristotelianism, 13-4, 22
Aristotle, 13-4, 16, 25
art:
  Byzantine, vii, 14, 59-115
  Classical Greek, 14, 60-1, 64, 70, 72
  Gothic, 60, 64-5
  Renaissance, 60-1, 70, 72, 76, 86, 94-5
ascesis, *see* spiritual training
Athanasios the Great, St., 18, 25, 35, 100
Athens, 17, 49, 63, 69
Athos, Mount, 48, 49, 79-84, 90, 92
attention, *see* inner attention

Barlaam, 15
Basil the Great, St., 21, 23-4, 25, 37, 43, 48, 56, 69, 87, 99-100, 110, 125
beautiful, the, 48, 51-2, 56, 60-2, 65, 69-70, 114, 128, 130, 131

beauty:
  physical, 69-70, 76-7, 114
  spiritual, 56, 69-70, 76-7, 82, 111, 114
Bergson, H., 38
body, 37, 50-1, 70, 101, 113, 131
Brehier, E., 13, 14
Brownlie, J., 111
Byzantium (Byzantine Empire), vii, 13, 59, 85-6

Callistos the Patriarch, *see* Xanthopoulos, Callistos
calm, 82, 94, 98, 100
canon (hymn), 109, 110
cares, 19, 54, 100
Cassian, St. John, 101
catechism, 22-3
Cavarnos, C., 122
Cavasilas, Nicholas, 15, 19, 24-5
change, inner, 53, 127, 131
Christ, 17, 18, 19, 21, 22, 24, 27, 28, 32, 35, 37, 44, 54, 55, 87, 88, 89, 92, 98, 99, 102, 103, 111, 112, 113, 114, 130-1
Christianity, 14, 16-8, 22, 23, 62, 64, 98
Chrysanthos, 106
Chrysostom, St. John, 17, 19, 41, 42, 43, 44, 82, 87, 99-100, 101, 103, 104, 110, 117
Clement of Alexandria, 17, 21-3, 24, 37, 125
Climacos, St. John, 19, 27, 31, 33, 41, 42, 43, 44, 77, 101, 102
Commandments, 28, 32, 33, 45-6, 52

concentration, 53-4, 55, 130, 131
conscience, 34-5, 37, 39, 40-7, 51, 52, 53, 57, 131
consciousness, 57-8, 127, 131
Constantine the Great, St., 13
Constantinople, 16, 49, 62, 65, 68, 86
contemplation, 20, 21, 36, 51, 57, 131
continence, 27, 30, 53
contrition, 32, 44, 76, 77, 98, 101, 102, 104, 129, 131
courage, 25, 30, 42, 113

Damascene, St. John, 15, 20, 24, 37, 50, 70, 99, 109, 110
Damascene, St. Peter, 33, 36, 39, 51, 54
Daniel, 24
David, 37, 98, 100
death, 23, 28, 54-5, 112, 113
deification, see theosis
Descartes, 38
Diadochos of Photike, St., 50
Dionysios of Fourna, 84
Dionysios the Areopagite, St., 28, 87
Dobrotolubiye, 49-50
Dolci, Carlo, 76
Dorotheos, Abba, 41, 42, 44, 45

eclecticism, 21-7
efforts, 53, 72, 101
effulgence, 56, 128, 131
empiricism, 30, 37-9
Ephraim the Syrian, St., 102
Epicurean philosophy, 22
eschatology, 23
Eucbologion, the Great, 109, 110
Eusebios, 17, 117
Evagrios the Monk, of Pontos, 57, 101
Evergetinos, 48
existential concern, 27-8

faith, 21, 26, 27, 28, 30, 31-3, 37, 39, 62
Fall, the, 30-1, 44
fantasies, 20, 55
fasting, 53, 77, 101
form, 25, 26
freedom, 50, 82
of the rational faculty, 51
of the will, 51-2
future life, 23-4, 27-8, 34

Gemistos, George, see Pletho
Gibbon, 85-6, 122
gladdening-sorrow, 44, 77, 132
God, 15, 17, 18, 19, 20, 21, 22, 25, 26, 28, 31, 32-3, 34, 35, 39, 54, 56, 57, 58, 61, 63, 70, 72, 74, 76, 95, 97, 98, 102, 111, 112, 113
grace, Divine, 31, 34, 37, 46, 52, 54, 56, 76, 77
Greco, El, see Theotokopoulos
Greece, 49
Gregory Nazianzen, St., 18, 19, 20, 25, 48, 69, 82, 99-100, 109
Gregory of Nyssa, St., 25, 35, 117, 125
Gregory the Sinaite, St., 15, 19, 20, 38, 51, 53
Gregory the Theologian, see Gregory Nazianzen

halo, 82, 95, 132
heart, 40, 44, 46, 54, 55, 56, 98, 102, 112, 132
heaven, 54, 72, 113
Hegel, 60
hell, 16, 43, 54
Heraclas, 17
hesychasm, 15, 132
Hesychios of Jerusalem, 20, 32, 37, 42
hope, 26, 27, 31, 42, 97, 112
holiness, 111

Hōrologion, 109, 110
Hort, F. J. A., 117
humility, 30, 32-3, 44, 64, 76, 77, 101, 102, 108
hymnody, 43, 78, 109-115

iconography, 16, 59, 64, 70, 72, 73-96, 110
iconostasis, 79, 123, 132
identification, 52, 132
Ignatios, St., 108
ignorance, 25, 31
illumination, 26, 32, 33-4, 37, 56-7, 132
imagination, 31, 41, 51, 52-3, 57, 74, 76, 79, 82, 132
individuality, 28-9
Ingres, 76
inner attention, 15, 19-20, 26, 31, 45, 46, 51, 52, 53, 54, 57-8, 100, 101-2, 105, 108, 129, 130, 131, 132
"in the image of God," 50, 132
"in the likeness of God," 50, 132
intuitionism, 30, 38
Isaiah, Abba, 33, 45, 46
isocratema, 105, 132
isocrats, 105
Italos, John, 16

Jeremiah of Sinai, 102
Jerome, St., 17, 87
Jesus Prayer, 55, 132
John of Karpathos, 46
John the Baptist, 87, 90
John the Evangelist, 18, 40, 99
joy, spiritual, 40, 42, 54, 98, 100
Judgment, 43, 52, 54
Justin Martyr, 17, 37, 87

Kelemen, Pal, viii, 85-94, 96
knowledge, 25, 26, 30-9, 42, 51, 55, 132
    according to nature, 36-7, 132

innate, natural, 34-7, 132
    spiritual, supernal, 37, 133
kontakion, 110, 129
Kontoglou(s), 73-8, **88**

Latin Church Fathers, 14, 87
love, 26; 27, 30, 31, 32, 34, 50, 56, 64, 98, 112, 114, 132
    of God, 15, 20, 32, 37, 44, 56, 97, 102
    of neighbor, 32, 44
    of virtue, 22, 56

Macarios of Corinth, St., 48
Macarios the Great, of Egypt, St., 28, 43, 44, 119
man, 30-1, 35-6, 43, 50, 53, 64
Mark the Ascetic, St., 31, 32, 46, 52, 119
Martyrikon, 112, 129
Mason, A. J., 18
matins, 110, 132
matter, 25, 26
Maximos the Confessor, St., 31-2, 33, 34, 37, 41, 102
meditation, 52, 53-5, 101, 132
meekness, 19, 20, 30, 32, 64, 113
Mēnaia, 109, 110
Meteora, 71
Michelis, P. A., 59-70
Moldavia, 49
Moliere, 60
monasticism, 15, 19-20, 26, 131
mode (musical), 109-10, 132
Moscow, 49
Moses, 24
music, 59, 77, 78, 97-108, 110
mysticism, 15, 18, 28-9, 46-7, 62, 73-4, 76
Mystra, 16

Neo-Platonism, 17
Nicodemos the Aghiorite, St., 42, 48
Nikephoros the Solitary, St., 57

Nilos the Ascetic, St., 17-8, 19, 101
non-attachment, 55, 132

Octōēchos, 43, 109
Origen, 17, 48

Palamas, St. Gregory, 15, 46-7, 50-1, 56
Palladios, 119
Panagiotopoulos, D. G., 104, 125
Panselinos, Manuel, 79-84
Pantainos, 22
Papadopoulos, G. I., 103
Paraklētikē, 43, 44, 109-10
Parios, Athanasios, 116
passionlessness, 27, 31, 32, 33-4, 36, 56, 132
passions, 31, 33, 34, 36, 38, 56, 100, 101, 113, 132
Paul the Apostle, 22, 26, 40, 41, 55, 84, 98-9, 100, 101, 102
Pentēkostarion, 109, 110
perfection, 21, 32, 39, 50, 57, 97
Peter the Apostle, 40-1
Petros the Peloponnesian, 106
Philemon, Abba, 33, 34
Philokalia, the, 48-58, 130
philosophy, vii, 13-39
    "external," 15-6, 19, 21, 22, 24-5, 30-1, 37-9, 131
    "internal," 15-39, 109, 132
Philotheos the Sinaite, 46
Picasso, 76
Plato, 13, 16, 23, 25-6, 31, 35, 69
Platonism, 13-4, 22
Pletho, 16
poetry, 59, 109
Porphyrios, 17
pragmatism, 30, 37-9
prayer, 21, 26, 31, 45, 51, 52, 55, 77, 100, 102, 132
    mental, 46, 53-8, 132
    of the heart, 46, 53-8, 133

pure, 44, 46, 53, 55, 133
preexistence, 16, 35
propaideia, 21, 22, 130
Psellos, Michael, 16
purification, 19, 32, 33-4, 45-6, 56, 72, 100, 101, 132

quiet, inner, 15, 19, 94, 100, 128

Raphael, 74, 76
rationalism, 16, 30, 37-9
Read, Herbert, 122
reason, 25-6, 33, 38, 40, 41, 50, 51, 53, 54, 132
    discursive, 31, 38, 51, 131
    intuitive, 31, 38, 51, 132
remorse, 42, 43
Reni, Guido, 76
Renoir, 76
resurrection, 33
revelation, 14, 16, 17, 21, 24, 25, 34, 37, 38
Romanos the Melodist, 109
Russia, 49

saints, 38, 42, 45, 50, 51, 54, 84, 97-8, 99, 110, 111, 113
salvation, 23, 27, 28, 51, 52, 99, 112, 113, 133
Santayana, 122
Scripture, 22, 23, 24-5, 35, 36, 40, 76, 98, 110
self-awareness, 57, 58
self-knowledge, 32, 39
self-observation, 39, 57
sin, 31, 35, 36, 43, 52, 57, 113, 133
sleep, spiritual, 42, 44, 57, 113, 133
socialism, 16
sociology, 16
Socrates, the historian, 108
soul, 25, 26, 29, 33, 34, 35, 37, 39, 44, 50-1, 56, 70, 72, 100, 133

spiritual guide, 55-6, 130
spiritual torpor, 101, 127
spiritual training, 46-7, 53, 133
Stethatos, Niketas, 28-9, 32, 33, 35-6, 44
Stoics, 16, 22, 27
sublime, the, 60-2, 64-5, 69
substance, 25, 133
suggestion, 52, 133
Symeon of Thessaloniki, 34, 70
Symeon the New Theologian, St., 18, 27-9, 31, 32, 33, 45, 54, 57, 99, 101-2, 109
Syria, 108

Tatakis, B., 13-6
Thalassios, Abba, 33, 34, 42, 43-4, 119
Theocletos Dionysiatis, 114
Theodore of Edessa, St., 36, 37, 51
Theodore the Studite, St., 70
Theodoretos, 125
Theoleptos, 55
theology, vii, 15-6, 18, 109
Theophan the Recluse, 49
theosis, 28-9, 37, 53, 57, 130
Theotokopoulos, Domenikos, 85-96
Theotokos, the, 75, 76, 95, 97, 110, 111, 113, 130-1
Thessaloniki, 66, 67, 79
The Way of A Pilgrim, 49

Tillyard, H. J. W., 103, 104, 125, 126
Tolstoi, L., 77-8
Tradition, Sacred, 25
Triōdion, 43, 109, 110
truth, 21-5, 30, 31, 32, 36, 51, 53, 77

unconsciousness, 34-6, 44-5, 57, 133

Velichkovsky, Paissy, 49
virtue, 21, 22, 23-6, 31-7, 42, 56, 72, 111, 113, 114
Vischer, Fr., 60
voluntary suffering, 53, 133

"Wakeful Fathers," 48, 57, 133
Wellesz, E., 103, 104, 126
will, 37, 39, 41, 51, 53, 133
wisdom, 17-20, 24, 25, 26, 27, 32, 33-4, 35, 64, 99, 100, 111, 114, 130
"work," 133
  bodily, 53
  spiritual, 53
"world," 36-7, 54, 133
worship, 19, 95, 97, 98, 99, 100, 105, 111

Xanthopoulos, Callistos, 20, 50, 54, 56
Xanthopoulos, Ignatios, 20, 56

DATE DUE

PRINTED IN U.S.A.